# To Die For

**25 Saturday Night Fright Flicks**

**Richard Cosgrove**

House of Darcy, London, UK

For Mum, who never discouraged my love of horror movies and who has always encouraged me to write.

# Order of Service

# Elegy

Blame it on John Travolta, it's all his fault. Danny Zuko himself is the root cause of this horror movie obsession that I've lived with for the best part of thirty years and you know what, I couldn't be happier.

So, what's Travolta got to do with this, I hear you ask? He's not exactly the poster boy for the horror genre, having appeared in only one bona fide horror movie over the years (unless you count Battlefield Earth, of course, but that's a different type of horror altogether), but as far as my story goes, one was enough.

In the summer of 1978 my family was living in Calgary, Canada and my parents had taken my brother and I to the cinema to see a musical called Grease, starring a young actor by the name of John Travolta. At the time I was unaware that he was tipped as the next big thing after his portrayal of ultra-hip disco dancer Tony Manero in Robert Stigwood's gritty Saturday Night Fever (which I eventually saw a couple of years later, but in the watered down, family friendly version), but seeing him strut his stuff on-screen in Grease, all slicked back hair, dark sunglasses and attitude, I thought he was cool. With a capital C-O-O-L.

Though Star Wars was still my favourite movie at this point, I couldn't really identify with the likes of Luke Skywalker, Ben Kenobi or Han Solo the way I did with Danny Zuko. Some guys just have that inherent cool factor, and to the eight year old me, Travolta was one of them. Maybe it's because Grease was set in a school, something I had a point of reference for, rather than some run down intergalactic Death Star somewhere in a galaxy far, far away that he had this profound effect on me, but whatever the reason, I was sold.

A couple of months later, I happened to catch a trailer for Brian De Palma's Carrie on TV which inevitably heavily pushed rising star Travolta's appearance in it. Not having the luxury of DVD or even video back in 1978, this was a rare opportunity to see more of my new hero, so I pestered my parents to the point of insanity to let me stay up and watch it even though it didn't start until nine o'clock at night, well past my usual bedtime.

Somehow I got them to agree and that was it - Carrie changed my life. Not only was it the first horror movie I ever watched that was in colour, and that didn't involve Dracula, the Mummy or Frankenstein, it also starred someone who I had actually heard of (as opposed to these guys with funny names like Karloff and Lugosi). On top of that it starred (well in a supporting role, but that was neither here nor there as far as I was concerned) one of the coolest guys around at the time, even cooler than Steve Austin, the Six Million Dollar Man who was a staple part of our Sunday evening family viewing, and in 1978 Lee Majors's recycled astronaut was pretty damn cool.

So, here I am nearly three decades and hundreds if not thousands of horror movies later, and I'm still as much in love with this blood soaked genre today as I was when I first fell for it in a big way back then. In that time I've seen a lot of great movies, some of which are included in this book, and a lot of truly awful ones, which perhaps should appear in another book of movies to avoid wasting ninety minutes of your life at a time with. Movies like Tobe Hooper's The Mangler, one of the most dreadful pieces of alleged entertainment I've ever had the misfortune to sit through. Thankfully Hooper seems to have regained his form in recent years with his involvement in Mick Gariss's inventive Masters of Horror anthology.

However, I digress. We're not here to discuss turkeys; we're here to celebrate two dozen and one of my favourite horror movies. Movies that I would heartily recommend for that most hallowed of horror rituals, the Saturday Night Fright Flick. All of the movies in this book are perfect, well in my humble, twisted opinion anyway, for a night on the sofa with your buddies, or your girl, or both if you're cool with that, a six-pack of cold beer, and a takeaway pizza (mine's a double pepperoni if you're buying).

Each of these movies have a special place in my dark heart, and stand up to repeated viewings, which is exactly what I've done before writing about them so as to get a fresh hit of the buzz that they give off as I put fingers to keyboard to wax lyrically about them.

Chances are, whatever type of horror movie fan you are, whether you occasionally dip your toes into the sticky red pool or dive right in and bathe in the stuff, you'll have seen at least some of these movies, so while I've tried to avoid any major spoilers, you will find some discussion of particular plot points and deaths, but hopefully these won't ruin a movie that you've yet to see. (I'll make it clear when there's a doozy of a revelation about to be revealed so you can grab a cushion or avert your eyes!)

In true masked maniac fashion, each movie has been carved up into succulent sections and served to you with a nice Chianti and a side order of fava beans. The five courses are; credits, a brief synopsis of the plot, my thoughts as to why I love that particular movie, my favourite scene from the movie, and a few titbits about the flick that you might not know.

OK, the beers are nicely chilled, the pizzas have arrived, so pull the curtains, kill the lights and let's hit play.

Bon appetit.

# 28 Days Later (2002)

Directed by:   Danny Boyle
Written by:    Alex Garland
Starring:      Cillian Murphy – Jim
               Naomie Harris – Selena
               Brendan Gleeson – Frank
               Megan Burns – Hannah
               Noah Huntley - Mark
               Christopher Ecclestone – Major Henry West

## Synopsis

A young bicycle courier wakes up alone in a hospital to discover that during the twenty-eight days he has been in a coma, a virus has swept throughout Great Britain, and possibly the world, turning people into the rage-fuelled 'infected'.

After wandering the deserted streets of London, he meets up with a handful of other survivors and they set off on a journey north towards the source of a radio transmission offering a cure for the infection. When they arrive there, however, it soon becomes apparent that the infected may not be their only problem.

## Why I Love This Movie

Though 28 Days Later was director Danny Boyle's debut genre flick, I was already very familiar with his work thanks to his first three movies, 1994's Shallow Grave, a dark thriller

7

about keeping secrets, 1996's Trainspotting, a harrowing portrait of a group of Scottish junkies, and his 2000 adaptation of one of my favourite novels, The Beach, written by Alex Garland.

Consequently when I read in Empire magazine that Boyle was to direct a horror movie based on a script that Garland was writing it piqued my interest somewhat. When I then found out it was to be a zombie movie set in London, my excitement level went right off the scale. Zombies! In London!

Although the early reports of this being the bastard son of Romero's dead trilogy were slightly wide of the mark in that there weren't actually going to be any zombies *per se*, the fact that the 'infected' are, well, infected by means of being bitten or through the transference of blood or saliva meant that in my eyes, and those of many a genre fan, this is a zombie movie by any other name.

Opening with newsreel footage of violence, rioting, and panic on the world's streets, Boyle cleverly foreshadows the as yet unseen effects of the 'Rage' virus that is about to be unleashed. The camera pulls back to reveal a chimpanzee strapped to a table, a couple of diodes implanted in its skull, being forced to watch the scenes of carnage and mayhem á *la* Alex de Large in Kubrick's A Clockwork Orange.

This is the first of many homages in the movie, which is effectively a love letter from Garland and Boyle to a genre that they have great affection for. Though largely bereft of any truly original ideas, 28 Days Later is a real treat for horror fans as it combines the best parts from several classic movies into a flick that moves along at a fair old lick and never really sags, save for a few scenes towards the end. Even then it takes nothing from the entertainment value, though.

As bicycle courier Jim comes around from his coma, having been hit by a car twenty-eight days earlier, he finds himself alone in a hospital. Taking a cue from the classic 1981 BBC Television version of John Wyndham's The Day of the Triffids, he wanders around the empty debris-strewn corridors looking for other people before taking to the streets in search of life (thankfully after getting dressed – Boyle kicks this whole sequence off with Jim butt naked in all his full-frontal glory).

It is here that Boyle pulls his masterstroke. As a native of London, an extended sequence of Jim walking through the capital's deserted streets, passing landmarks that are normally bustling with tourists at all hours, always unsettles me. These are streets and areas that I'm very familiar with and have walked through myself many times. I guess this must be what natives of New York, Los Angeles or Tokyo feel when they see their hometowns destroyed on a regular basis by fires, floods, earthquakes or Godzilla.

The scenes of post-apocalyptic empty streets, hoardings filled with 'Missing' posters (the image of which was brought sharply back into my head in the aftermath of the 7th July 2005 suicide bombings in London when the outside of Kings Cross railway station was plastered with similar notices) and Jim's desperate echoing cries of 'hello' would have appealed to my horror movie sensibilities whatever city they were set in, but the fact this was in London (my manor, as it were) still sends shivers down my spine whenever I watch it now.

Throughout the first half of the movie Boyle very convincingly conveys the feeling of London as a vast necropolis. Cars are abandoned in the middle of intersections (one of which is the source of a cheap but effective scare), newspapers and bank notes litter the streets, and the aftermath of the violence and panic that has swept the population is very much in evidence, including an overturned double decker bus in Westminster and a message scrawled on the wall of a church urging 'repent – the end is extremely fucking nigh'.

With no electricity, the wide shots of the city are grey and lifeless. Even the usually perpetually turning London Eye, the huge Ferris wheel that towers above the Houses of Parliament, has stopped. This muted palette makes the two main splashes of colour on the landscape all the more striking when they occur, the first when a petrol station explodes and the second when we see the beacon that heralds the arrival of the movie's second act.

While the shots of Jim roaming alone through the streets of London like an Anglicised version of Charlton Heston in 1971's The Omega Man are chilling and compelling, the movie really comes into its own through the performances of its leads, all of whom bring an authenticity and gravity to their roles.

Cillian Murphy is extremely convincing as Jim, the man who has woken up to find everything he thought he knew has changed. After meeting up with fellow survivors Selena and Mark, who rescue him from a horde of the infected, his struggle to comprehend that there is no longer a government, an army or even a police force and that his parents are almost certainly dead is very believable, as is the development arc that his character goes through from the initially mild-mannered potential victim to a hardened survivor who will do whatever it takes to stay alive and protect his friends.

Naomie Harris as Selena is another great piece of casting by Boyle, who wisely opted to go with a largely unknown cast. Initially a nihilistic survivor who considers life as she once knew it to be a distant memory, and that 'staying alive is as good as it gets', she undergoes her own development in the opposite direction to that of Jim's. Moving from being ready to turn on her companions 'in a heartbeat' if they become infected, which she does with a frightening gusto early in the movie, she slowly realises that there is more to this new world than merely surviving.

Veteran actor Brendan Gleeson, best known as Professor Alastor 'MadEye' Moody from 2005's Harry Potter and the Goblet of Fire, is superb as Frank, an everyman caught up in an extraordinary situation. Having lost his wife early on in the outbreak, he has steadfastly remained in their flat trying to do best for his daughter Hannah by raiding the other flats for much needed water, even going so far as to set up hundreds of buckets on the roof of the block along with a tarpaulin that he hopes will capture water because he saw someone do it on television. (To emphasise the dwindling supply, there is a subtle shot of a goldfish swimming around in a bowl containing barely two inches of water.) Realising he must protect his daughter at all costs, he set

10

up his makeshift beacon and is overjoyed when Jim and Selena come calling.

The believable characters lift 28 Days Later head and shoulders above other similar apocalyptic movies and along with the scenes of dead London are the reason why this movie is a firm favourite of mine.

Megan Burns plays Hannah not as the usual precocious, sex-mad, weed smoking teen that recent American horror movies are so fond of embracing, but rather as a resourceful young woman who is coping remarkably well with the loss of her mother and adapting to the unfolding new world. In fact, as she shows in a couple of key scenes, she may just be more astute and capable of survival than the adults who are supposedly there to save her.

Less effective are the soldiers that turn up in the third act, led competently but uninspiringly by Christopher Eccleston's Major Henry West, and this is where Boyle loses momentum a little by riffing a touch too much on his Day of the Dead influences, but ultimately failing to capture the claustrophobia or tension of George Romero's 1985 classic. This final section does, however, raise an interesting theory as to the extent of the outbreak (which provides the basis of 2007's excellent sequel 28 Weeks Later), and also brings about a dramatic change in the behaviour of one of the leads which draws some ironic parallels to the infected themselves.

Overall, though, Boyle and Garland have managed between them to create a very satisfying Saturday Night Fright Flick, just about walking that fine line between homage and rip-off in their reinterpretation of some very familiar elements and situations from some of my favourite genre movies. Whether riffing on various elements of Romero's Dead Trilogy (at the time, before 2006's Land of the Dead), The Omega Man, or The Day of the Triffids, it's apparent that this movie is shot with a genuine love for the source material rather than being a cynical exercise in plagiarism.

A final mention here must go to the zombies, sorry, the 'infected' themselves. This is the one element of Garland's script that does break new ground, and would go on to influence, among others, Zack Snyder's 2004 remake of Romero's Dawn of the Dead. There are no slowly shuffling, easy to dodge cadavers in 28 Days Later. Instead we get 'Rage' fuelled human beings who are hell-bent on taking a bite out of their fellow man, and who can, and do, run at full pelt in order to chow down on their victims.

This is demonstrated particularly effectively in a scene set in a tunnel as our heroes change a tire on their vehicle (inspiringly cast as a black London cab). After a pack of rats flee past them, we see first the shadows of a running mob and then the infected themselves as they swiftly close in, clambering over wrecked cars with the speed and agility of wild animals.

The bottom line – this is the best non-zombie zombie movie of recent years, despite its relatively small shortcomings.

**My Favourite Scene**

I'm going to cheat a little here and choose the entire sequence between Jim leaving the hospital and entering the church (hey, it's my book!).

Seeing Jim walking past landmarks recognisable to anyone who knows anything about London, calling out 'hello' only for his voice to echo around the deserted streets, is supremely unsettling. Jim's feelings of confusion and isolation are further accentuated by the soundtrack. Beginning in silence and then slowly introducing a lone guitar, it proceeds to build to a frenetic jig as he darts this way and that, picking up handfuls of money that he doesn't yet realise is completely worthless.

The images of a deserted Tottenham Court Road, Westminster Bridge (which in another iconic moment once had Dr Who's mortal enemies The Daleks glide across many years before), and Piccadilly Circus with its hoardings full of 'Missing' posters now always come back to me whenever I'm in one of those locations. Chilling stuff.

**Did You Know That...**

Christopher Ecclestone went on to become the ninth incarnation of Dr Who, portraying the time lord for thirteen episodes before bowing out and handing the role over to David Tennant. He also turned up in the superb Heroes series as Claude, a man who can turn himself invisible.

Former Boyle collaborators Leonardo DiCaprio and Ewan MacGregor were both considered for the role of Jim.

While filming the mansion scenes, the crew spent a lot of time in a pub called The Wooden Spoon in Downton, Wiltshire. When they left they presented the owner with one of the bodies from the execution scene, which can apparently still be found sitting at a table there to this day.

Good-looking women were hired to persuade motorists to be cooperative while Boyle temporarily blocked off roads in order to shoot scenes of empty London streets.

None of the footage in the opening montage is genuine. It was recreated based on scenes that Garland and Boyle had seen of social unrest that had occurred in Sierra Leone and Rwanda.

Megan Burns now goes by the name of Betty Curse and fronts a goth-rock band of the same name. Check them out at www.myspace.com/bettycursemusic.

# A Nightmare On Elm Street (1984)

Directed by:   Wes Craven
Written by:    Wes Craven
Starring:       Robert Englund – Fred Krueger
               Heather Langencamp – Nancy Thompson
               John Saxon – Lt Thompson
               Ronee Blakley – Marge Thompson
               Amanda Wyss – Tina Gray
               Nick Corri – Rod Lane
               Johnny Depp – Glen Lantz

## Synopsis

A group of teenagers are suffering from bad dreams in which a disfigured man wearing a fedora, and with knives for fingers, is stalking them. No one takes them seriously until they start dying in the real world and it becomes apparent that their parents know more about the killer than they originally let on.

## Why I Love This Movie

I was fourteen years old when A Nightmare On Elm Street came out, and slightly too young to pass for eighteen and be able to see it at the cinema. (The following year I did manage to get in to see Fright Night, another 18-certificate movie, and my big screen horror movie cherry was popped.) I do remember the TV ads captivating me, though, with their promise of dark alleyways and a gravel voiced killer who from the fleeting glimpses we were given seemed to be the coolest thing I'd ever seen at that point.

In due course the movie was released on VHS video, and my friend Brian's dad rented it from their local video store. Being the horror movie fanatics that we were, we naturally didn't just want to see this movie, we wanted our very own copies. So, one evening Brian and his older brother Darren carried their video recorder down the street to my house, no mean feat in those days, what with it being the size of a small car, along with a dozen or so leads. After a great deal of trial and error we managed to hook the two machines up and get the movie transferring from one to the other.

The technical bit sorted, we sat on the sofa in anticipation of having our respective worlds rocked by Freddy Krueger. To say we were blown away is an understatement. Nightmare made a huge impression on me, further cementing my passion for horror that had been sparked by Carrie and fuelled by The Thing, Zombie Flesh Eaters and The Texas Chain Saw Massacre. The opening sequence alone where we see, in great detail, Freddy making his glove, inspired me to attempt a similar feat in our metalwork class at school. I fashioned some crudely cut dull blades out of a sheet of aluminium and attached them to a bright yellow gardening glove that I had liberated from our shed. It didn't look quite the same as Freddy's but it was close enough for me.

I even persuaded Mum to get one of her friends to knit me a Freddy sweater with the red and green horizontal hoops, not revealing why I wanted that particular colour scheme or pattern, just that I thought it would be cool. Finally, to top off my outfit I borrowed one of Dad's old hats. Not quite the battered fedora that Freddy wore but, again, it was close enough for me.

So why did this film have such an impact on me? Easy answer. It was genuinely scary and Freddy was without a shadow of a doubt the creepiest and most menacing movie monster that I had come across at that point, and in many ways remains in that top spot when judging him by the merits of the first film alone.

Nowadays Freddy has a reputation as being a wise-cracking cartoon villain, particularly after his rough and tumble with Crystal Lake's prodigal son in 2003's Freddy vs Jason, but back in 1984 he was plain old Fred Krueger and still an undiluted, genuinely frightening, child killing maniac (though we wouldn't discover that he was the bastard son of a hundred of them until the third movie in the series).

There's not a single witty remark or nod to the camera in Nightmare. Robert Englund plays Freddy as straight as a die and is all the more menacing for it. When we get our first proper look at him, as Tina wanders out into the alley behind her house after someone wakes her (or so we think) by throwing stones at her window, the sight of his horrifically burned face and impossibly long outstretched arms, blades screeching down a metal garage door in a shower of sparks, is genuinely creepy.

He exudes menace and I thought he was the *crème de la crème* of movie bad guys when I first saw this scene and, sequels aside, I still do. While I love everything about Freddy, even his very lame and mercifully brief stint on MTV around the time of Dream Warriors, I consider the first movie and the five sequels that followed it to be two very different sides of the same coin. Wes Craven's New Nightmare is a whole different ball game again, and was an effective return to the undiluted horror of the original movie.

Though the character of Freddy has become more of a co-median than a maniac over the years, I am eternally grateful to Robert Englund for continually reprising what is undeniably his role. No one else could bring the personality to it that he can, and for anyone else to even try would in my humble opinion be madness. Some roles are so intrinsically linked to certain actors that to try and fill their shoes is a hopeless task. Imagine anyone except Doug Bradley playing Pinhead. It just wouldn't work. Even the silent masked killers have their own characteristics.

For me, Dick Warlock will always be the definitive Michael Myers, and just to prove that for every rule there is an exception, though he didn't pull on the overalls and hockey mask until Part

VII: The New Blood, Kane Hodder is my Jason Voorhees of choice, and that of a good number of the horror community.

One man does not a great movie make, though, and props must be given to the rest of cast who made their characters believable, and more importantly for a horror movie, into people that we actually cared about. Heather Langenkamp made us believe in Nancy Thompson, so much so that there was elation amongst Nightmare fans, myself included, when she returned first in 1987's Dream Warriors and then again in 1994's New Nightmare.

John Saxon, also enthusiastically welcomed back in Dream Warriors, brought a certain weight to his role as Nancy's father, especially in his Dirty Harry moment when he apprehends Rod Lane with a big ass gun, and Ronee Blakley while initially appearing a little bland as Marge Thompson, came into her own when extrapolating Fred Krueger's back story and revealing Elm Street's dark secret. Amanda Wyss was convincing as Tina, making celluloid history as Freddy's first on-screen kill, and some guy called Johnny Depp put in a competent performance, after moving from Jump Street to Elm Street.

Englund aside, though, the real star of this picture was Wes Craven. Having cut his teeth on classics Last House On The Left and The Hills Have Eyes, Nightmare saw him break through into the mainstream, effectively kick-starting the concept of the horror movie franchise for the 1980s. Halloween and Friday the 13th had been slowly building their franchise fan base for a few years before Nightmare came out, but Freddy Krueger captured the imagination of the general public in a way that Jason and Michael hadn't been able to. By the time Nightmare first came out, I'd seen the first two Halloweens and the first and third Friday the 13th movies but with the exception of John Carpenter's original Halloween, they hadn't really freaked me out as such.

Freddy Krueger did, though, and I think it was largely because he actually spoke, and so had that human quality that his maniacal peers lacked. Jason and Michael were big, hulking scary killers, but they were silent. Krueger on the other hand scared the hell out of me when he whispered Tina's name during the opening sequence where he stalks her through the boiler room, and that made it all the more terrifying. It made it personal.

Michael and Jason were like a force of nature. Big, destructive, unstoppable. Freddy, by virtue of the fact that he spoke, and that we knew that he had effectively been murdered himself by the Elm Street parents, was a much more human proposition. When we first meet him in Tina's back yard and she begs "Please God," his response of holding up his razor gloved hand and replying "This.....is God" is both terrifying and chilling. Jason and Michael were hard-wired automatons, but Freddy knew exactly what freaked us out and used it against us.

One thing that has surprised me about Nightmare over the years, and something it has in common with Tobe Hooper's classic 1974 The Texas Chain Saw Massacre, is that there isn't actually that much gore in the movie. In fact, including Marge Thompson's lame dummy through the window death right at the end (in fact her second demise of the flick), there are only five kills in the entire movie, three of which are bloodless. The only time we see any of the red stuff is when Tina is dragged up the wall and across the ceiling near the beginning of the movie, and when Johnny Depp becomes a bloody Mount Vesuvious towards the end. Rod Lane is bloodlessly hanged in his cell, and Marge Thompson is turned into a char-grilled tailor's dummy before sinking into her bed.

This doesn't hurt the movie in the least, however. Craven constructed a scary, tense, intelligent horror movie with Nightmare, and the ever-diminishing sequels and pale imitators that followed can take nothing away from his achievement.

**My Favourite Scene**

The scene in Tina's backyard when we first meet Freddy. The sight of him sauntering down the alley, impossibly long arms stretched out, finger knives scraping down the metal garage door, freaked me out the first time I saw it. In subsequent movies Freddy became our best bud, giving us a nod, a wink and a wise crack while slashing his way through waves of nubile teens, but when we first met him there was no doubt whatsoever that not only was he genuinely scary, but he was dangerous with it.

Freddy mark one was as serious as cancer about taking you out, and because of this the original Nightmare stands head and shoulders above the increasingly humourous sequels.

## Did You Know That...

Wes Craven appeared in the first Scream movie – he played a janitor called Fred who wore a red and green sweater and a fedora.

Demi Moore and Courteney Cox were among over 200 actresses who auditioned for the role of Nancy.

Freddy's glove appears hanging on a cellar wall in Sam Raimi's Evil Dead II. This was a nod to the trailer for The Evil Dead playing on the television in Nightmare.

The title of the movie, A Nightmare On Elm Street was allegedly inspired by the fact that President John F Kennedy was assassinated on Elm Street in Dallas, Texas on 22 November 1963.

Nightmare inspired a whole host of spin off ventures, including video games, several comic series, and even a television series in which Englund reprised his role as Freddy in a largely Cryptkeeper capacity.

# Alien (1979)

Directed by: Ridley Scott
Written by: Dan O'Bannon
Starring: Sigourney Weaver - Ripley
Tom Skerrit - Dallas
Ian Holm - Ash
Veronica Cartwright - Lambert
John Hurt - Kane
Harry Dean Stanton - Brett
Yaphet Kotto - Parker

**Synopsis**

Awakened from their cryogenic sleep by a distress signal, the crew of the Nostromo investigate a nearby planetoid, discovering a derelict ship with a hold full of giant eggs. One of the crew, Kane, is attacked and subsequently transferred back to the ship's medical bay with an alien attached to his face.

Some time later the alien detaches itself and turns up dead, leaving Kane apparently fully recovered. As he and the rest of the crew eat dinner later, however, he has a seizure and a small alien bursts violently through his ribcage and disappears into the depths of the ship. As the crew desperately try to locate it it begins to grow, and starts feeding on the crew.

## Why I Love This Movie

My earliest memory of Ridley Scott's haunted house in space movie is of seeing the trailer for it in front of whichever horror movie my friend Nick and I were watching on that particular Saturday afternoon. Unlike most of the trailers at the time, which were beginning to feature either masked killers in the wake of Halloween's success or gigantic bugs and slugs of various species, for the first thirty seconds of this one it did, well, not much at all. For nearly half a minute, an eternity in the world of trailers, it just alternated between a tracking shot across the surface of a planet that looked as though a three year old had built it in playschool, and a close up of an egg. While this went on, white lines slowly formed the word Alien at the top of the screen. In silence, no less.

Now this should have been the most boring start to a trailer ever, and should have had us hitting the fast forward button (if it didn't require virtually standing on to operate it as was the norm back in the day), but as Scott would prove in the movie proper, there's nothing like silence and seemingly mundane situations to lull you into a false sense of security.

Flashing up the now classic "In Space No-one Can Hear You Scream" tag line accompanied by a bloodcurdling, if contradictory, scream of terror, Scott suddenly hit us with a quick fire montage of claustrophobic corridors, people running, shots of vast alien spaceships, more people running, and then at the very end a brief glimpse of what was at that point possibly the scariest and most awesome creature that I had ever seen. Or to be more accurate, not seen, thanks to the split second that it was on screen. No matter how much we rewound and freeze-framed the creature, it remained a blur of motion and teeth, but the trailer had done its work. We were desperate to see this movie. Not next month, not next week, but now!

After what seemed like an eternity, and which occasionally was back then thanks to movies sometimes not being made available on the new video format for months or even years, we finally got to load the rented VHS tape into the huge video playing machine, and with our chests close to bursting point with anticipation, we hit the play button.

Alien didn't disappoint, and has continued to deliver every single time that I've watched it over the years. Ridley Scott took Dan O'Bannon's tight-as-a-drum script and fashioned a creepy, atmospheric, scary and at times brutal movie. It's a slow burner, but when it does explode at periodic intervals, it does so with enthusiasm and gusto (not to mention guts in its most visceral and memorable sequence).

For the best part of the first hour, Scott lets the movie drift along at a leisurely pace, introducing us to the seven crew members and roaming the Nostromo's endless corridors. The strongest of these characters are Yaphet Kotto's Parker and Harry Dean Stanton's Brett, the underling maintenance men and the crew's very own Laurel and Hardy. Not because there are many laughs in this picture, because there aren't, but because of their body language, Parker's smart mouth and in your face attitude, and Brett's almost mute existence, save for a few lines of dialogue, most of which consist of the word "Right", give their characters real life and invite our emotional investment in their well being.

Though I didn't see it coming the first time around, on subsequent viewings it's obvious from the get go that Ian Holm's Ash isn't all that he seems. Check out his ultra stiff posture in the cryogenic sleep tubes, his familiarity with the minutiae of the contracts when Parker is angling for a larger percentage, and his odd little run on the spot twenty-two minutes into the movie, almost as if he's trying the manoeuvre out for the first time to see what it feels like. When he finally does go off in the second half of the movie, the look on Holm's face is superb, his emotionless determination to force a rolled up magazine down Ripley's throat sending genuine chills down my spine.

Sigourney Weaver's Ripley needs no introduction, of course, but this isn't the Ripley we know and love from Aliens and beyond. This Ripley begins life as an unremarkable member of the crew, just looking to do her job with the minimum of fuss, and knowing what we know now (from the additional footage in the 1992 Special Edition), just wanting to get home. It's only when she is forced to step up to the plate and undergoes her metamorphosis from Warrant Officer to Alien Ass-Kicker that the character really comes alive. The exact moment this happens is captured in a beautiful shot of her eyes hardening just before she lets rip with a flamethrower in the now infamous deleted scene (restored for 2003's Director's Cut) where she comes across a cocooned Dallas and Brett towards the end of the movie.

The real star of this show, however, is Swiss artist H R Giger, or rather his twisted imagination. Famous for his erotic biomechanical art, his designs put Alien head and shoulders above any other creature movie, with the sets alone drawing my breath with their horrific beauty. The organic interior of the Space Jockey's ship is simply stunning, lined with bones in a style very reminiscent of the Catacombs in Paris, where six million bodies are buried, their tibias, fibulas and skulls stacked several feet deep and arranged into intricate patterns for miles on end.

The Space Jockey itself is deserving of a mention, a creature unlike anything I'd seen on screen before and much bigger than the three crew members who examine its blown out ribs. This not only foreshadows the events to come, it also very effectively conveys a sense that these little human beings have stumbled upon something far bigger than they can conceive, a feeling that is reinforced when they move on into the egg chamber, vast and cavernous, lined with row upon row upon row of eggs covered with an eerie luminous blue mist.

And then there's the creature itself, the eponymous alien. Not content with just one menacing killing machine, Giger devised an entire life cycle for it, managing to tap into several primal human fears in the process. First up is the facehugger, a spider like creature that wraps its acid filled appendages around your face, effectively suffocating you, and forcing itself down your throat in a bizarre alien rape in order to keep you alive.

24

Then there's the chestburster, which emulates the human birthing process, albeit taking a more direct and painful route to the outside world and playing on the fear of having something alien growing inside us. Finally there's the classic insect-like alien in all its adult glory, playing extremely effectively on our fear of, well, being hunted down and ripped apart by huge insect-like alien creatures.

The sets and aliens alone wouldn't make this a classic movie, though, and this is where Ridley Scott comes into his own, breathing life into the ship and turning the tension up to unbearable levels at times. The sequence where Brett goes looking for Jones, the ship's other non-human passenger, plays out for some four minutes, the camera slowly stalking him as he searches the dark corridors for the cat, chains rattling lazily in the artificial breeze, water dripping Chinese water torture style from the ceiling. We just know that something is going to happen here, and it does, eventually, but not before we've sat hovering uncomfortably on the edge of our seats for a while.

Likewise the scene with Dallas in the air vents, trying to flush out the alien. Putting us right in his face, and cranking up the claustrophobia in the process, Scott slams the tension levels into the red as we see the blip representing the alien appear on the monitor, and then move slowly, slowly towards him, his eyes wide, desperately trying to see where the creature is.

Despite being well into its third decade as I write this, though many have tried to emulate Scott's movie, none have come close to creating the heady mix of believable characters, oppressive atmosphere, high tension and crucially, an alien as horrific or as scary as Giger's ingenious creation.

**My Favourite Scene**

The classic and infamous chestburster scene. For the first fifty minutes of the movie Scott has lulled us into a false sense of security, delivering a sedately paced story with few scares or shocks up to this point. As we join the crew at the table with the apparently recovered Kane, a scene echoing the first crew gathering, we have no idea of the surprise that is just moments away. Suddenly Kane goes into convulsions and as he is being held down on the table by Dallas and Parker the confusion of the scene stops dead as Kane screams and blood explodes from his chest.

As the crew step back, trying to comprehend what has just happened, Scott gives us a moment to share their confusion before delivering the scene's coup de grace as something bursts out of Kane's chest, splattering the crew with blood in the process. We get a momentary extreme close up of a snake-like creature, all teeth and slime, coiled in his chest and then it's gone, shooting across the table and disappearing out of the door.

Not only does this scene feel authentic, largely due to the fact that the actors were not told exactly what was about to happen, witness Veronica Cartwright's very real expression of shock and disgust as she is covered in blood, it also provides a perfect transition from the sedate, slow burn of the first half of the movie to the tense, brutal second half.

**Did You Know That...**

Sigourney Weaver's real first name is Susan.

Peter Mayhew, best known as the wookie Chewbacca, was beaten to the part of the alien by Masai graphic artist Bolaji Badejo, who was discovered in a pub by one of the casting directors.

The Space Jockey prop was twenty-six feet tall, but made to appear larger on screen by using three children to portray Lambert, Dallas and Kane in the scene. Two of the children were Ridley Scott's.

Writer Dan O'Bannon also wrote the screenplay for 1985's horror comedy Return of the Living Dead.

London's Trocadero Centre was home to Alien War for a few years in the Nineties, where you could be stalked through a Weyland Yutani complex by an escaped Alien.

# Cabin Fever (2002)

Directed by:   Eli Roth

Written by:   Eli Roth and Randy Pearlstein

Starring:      Rider Strong – Paul
Jordan Ladd – Karen
James DeBello – Bert
Cerina Vincent – Marcy
Joey Kern - Jeff

## Synopsis

Five college friends head up into the woods to spend a relaxing week together after finishing school. When one of them contracts a mysterious flesh-eating virus, however, the group begins to fragment as they try to survive both the virus and their growing mistrust of one another.

## Why I Love This Movie

When Eli Roth first announced his arrival on the horror movie scene in the pages of Fangoria, he promised that Cabin Fever would be a return to the good old days of the scary, gory horror movies of the 1970s. This would be no toothless genre flick like FX maestro Tom Savini's largely bloodless (thanks to the MPAA) 1991 remake of George A Romero's classic 1967 zombie masterpiece Night of the Living Dead. Cabin Fever was to be a celebration of the best things that the Texas Chain Saw Massacre, The Hills Have Eyes and their ilk had been all about.

The late 1980s had seen our beloved horror movies turned into an endless parade of horror comedies, witness Freddy Krueger's increasing dependence on 'Schwarzenegger' lines as he sliced and diced his way through the annual teen body count (it's sometimes difficult to remember that he was genuinely scary back in the first Nightmare on Elm Street movie). This wasn't completely a bad thing – 1995's Return of the Living Dead remains a classic to this day – but thanks to it becoming the only option on the menu it left us genre fans missing the sumptuous blood feasts of the good old days.

Thankfully, Wes Craven used his gravitas and reputation (intact despite the abysmal Vampire in Brooklyn debacle) to get his Scary Movie project off the ground. Better known as Scream, he managed to demonstrate that you could actually market a movie *as* a horror movie and still have it become a success. As Roth himself notes, before Scream heralded the new wave of 'ironic' horror, if a bone fide genre movie like Jonathon Demme's 1991 Silence of the Lambs broke the $100 million box office barrier it suddenly became a thriller.

Thankfully new kid on the block Roth delivers on his promise, and with an enthusiasm that few directors manage to convey, particularly with their debut picture. Roth doesn't so much wear his influences on his sleeve as strut around in a custom made suit like he was cock-o-the-walk. Cabin Fever has attracted its fair share of naysayers, but the truth is that he has fashioned a movie that is perfect Saturday Night Fright Flick fodder.

No, it's not very original in its premise, and yes, the characters are by the numbers but those who have slated Roth for these points have missed the point of this flick entirely. He set out to make a loving homage to the films that both he and I grew up with and love to death, and with that goal in mind succeeds admirably.

This movie really works for me on several levels. As I've stated in several of the other pieces in this book, I absolutely love movies with an isolated backwoods setting, and while this isn't a variation on the inbred mountain man scenario usually associated with these locales, Roth is clearly also a fan of this type of movie, and even throws in a knowing nod to Deliverance, as the teens drive up to a remote general store and encounter an obviously backwards backwoods child sitting on a porch swing, a not so subltle homage to the banjo playing boy in the classic Burt Reynolds movie.

This isn't the only acknowledgement of his roots. Later in the movie an infected dog pursues one of the unfortunate teens, at which point Roth switches to steadicam POV, with a red filter no less, indulging his Sam Raimi Evil Dead fantasies. There's also a brief scene in a hospital at the end as one of the kids is wheeled along a corridor on a gurney. He turns his head to look into a room and sees a man in a bunny suit presiding over an operation, a clear reference to Richard Kelly's 2001 classic Donnie Darko. (The icing on the cake for this reference comes in the credits which list the actor (or actress) playing the 'Bunny Man' as 'we will never tell'.)

I also love the whole infection angle, which again is hardly a new thing, and is present in many of my favourite movies from Romero's Dead Quadrilogy (blame the Alien marketing people for this new word) to Danny Boyle's 28 Days Later, Cronenberg's Shivers, and Mick Garris's ambitious adaptation of Stephen King's classic The Stand.

Roth understands the value of good foreshadowing and employs this in varying degrees of subtlety to create a certain inevitability in the movie. Early on, two of the characters, textbook jocks Jeff and Bret, bet each other that they will drink nothing but beer for the rest of the week. Not long afterwards, having been introduced to an infected hermit who asks for help but who the teens manage to accidentally set on fire, we see his body face down in a reservoir from which the local drinking water is sourced.

Latterly we see another couple of characters drink a cup of tea and a glass of water respectively, though Roth doesn't draw attention to these actions. Instead he gives the audience enough credit to figure out the significance of these seemingly irrelevant actions.

The scene at the store with the Deliverance kid is a very subtle foreshadow too, as the kid bites Bret's hand when he offers to shake, provoking Bret to suggest that a sign be put up to warn customers about the kid. Later in the movie the kid strikes again, but with a very different outcome.

Despite the perceptions of Cabin Fever being a dumb horror movie, Roth displays his astute observations of how groups in society are quick to turn on each other in times of crisis. When one of the teens is discovered to be suffering from the effects of the fever, the other four are quick to enforce a quarantine, effectively imprisoning their infected friend in a shed so that the infection doesn't spread. The infected teen, however, is fully aware of what is going on, and the sense of betrayal that she feels comes across devastatingly in her comments and the look on her face.

The fragmentation of the five's friendship is superbly handled, each of them suspecting the other, and even inspecting each other's bodies in a scene reminiscent of the couch scene in John Carpenter's The Thing. Before long they won't eat together, sleep together or trust each other. Even their attempts to find help are fragmented, with one of the girls heading off alone while the two jocks head off in a different direction.

Being a horror movie, and bearing his promise in mind, when it comes to the gore quota Roth comes through in spades. Thanks to the work of the KNB group, the various stages of the infection are realistically rendered. The bloody vomit, infectious sores, dead dog and towards the end of the movie, spectacularly liquid head explosion are all executed with aplomb. While not as graphic and stomach churning as his follow up movie Hostel (and the slightly disappointing sequel), there are a couple of scenes in Cabin Fever that had me wincing, in particular the slow reveal of some nasty open sores as one of the girls shaves her legs in the bath. Like the hand in Carrie, even though I know exactly what's going to happen it still makes me grimace every time I watch it.

This might all sound very grim, but the other vital ingredient Roth has brought to the party, along with the lashings of 1970s style gore, is a sense of humour. I have to admit that part of me thinks that the movie might have been much stronger without the humour, but it could be argued that Roth went in that direction with Hostel, and to devastating effect. Cabin Fever's humour does work well, though, so I'm more than happy to it for the almost tongue-in-cheek homage to the 1970s that it is.

Deputy Winston Olsen, played with over the top gusto by Guiseppe Andrews should really be one of those characters that are annoying in a movie like this, but somehow Roth turns him into a likeable halfwit, whose obsession with partying actually makes him quite endearing rather than a pain in the ass.

This love of partying sets up another comedic moment late on in the movie as one of the main characters comes across Deputy Winston cutting some rug with a group of under age drinkers. One of the group attempts to hit the infected teen with an acoustic guitar but misses and instead hits another party goer in the face, driving a harmonica down his throat, setting up a couple of shots of him staggering around making harmonica noises as he tries to breath. Wonderfully pitch black humour in the Airplane / Monty Python vein. (Check out the Python's Salad Days sketch for a hernia-inducing example of gory comedy.)

The final few moments also showcase Roth's twisted sense of humour, providing a montage of irony that the seasoned genre viewing can't help but smile at. Yes, it's overload and in many ways completely ridiculous, but the bottom line is that as a fan of 1970s horror movies it made me laugh, and Roth should be applauded for having the balls to stick to his vision.

The bottom line with Cabin Fever is that despite its flaws, and it does have them, this is ninety minutes of entertainment that doesn't pull its punches. Roth trashes the 1990s horror taboos and includes sex, nudity, gore, and even one apparently racist comment early in the movie that he cleverly pays off in the final moments in a manner that the lame Scary Movie series would dearly love to replicate.

Cabin Fever is what I like to call a 'two beer' movie, i.e. sink a couple of cold ones, put your brain in neutral and just enjoy the ride.

In short, a perfect Saturday Night Fright Flick.

## My Favourite Scene

Having been bitten for the second time by Deliverance boy Dennis, one of the teens is pursued back to the cabin by a trio of armed men who are intent on 'stopping the problem' of the infection. Upon reaching the cabin, they find that the two surviving teens are waiting for them and a showdown ensues that is worthy of the final shoot out in Tarrantino's Reservoir Dogs.

This brief but violent sequence ends with a homage to Romero's Dawn of the Dead by way of a nice ear/screwdriver interface, and also an allusion to the 'what's in the case' mystery of Pulp Fiction as screwdriver boy struggles to open a mysterious box just before he gets nailed.

## Did You Know That...

The inspiration for the flesh-eating virus in Cabin Fever came from a real incident that happened to Eli Roth. While helping to clean out a barn during a trip to Iceland, Roth had such a bad allergic reaction to the rotting hay that his face broke out in bloody sores.

Cabin Fever was the most profitable horror movie released in 2003.

Jordan Ladd appears briefly in Hostel Part II, and also in Roth's fake trailer for Thanksgiving that he shot for Robert Rodriguez and Quentin Tarrantino's Grindhouse project.

# Candyman (1992)

Directed by:   Bernard Rose
Written by:    Bernard Rose (based on Clive Barker's
               short story 'The Forbidden')
Starring:      Virginia Madsen – Helen Lyle
               Tony Todd – Candyman/Daniel Robitaille
               Xander Berkeley – Trevor Lyle
               Kasi Lemmons – Bernadette Walsh
               Vanessa Williams – Anne-Marie McCoy
               DeJuan Guy – Jake
               Carolyn Lowery - Stacy

**Synopsis**

While researching a thesis on urban legends, Helen Lyle learns that the residents of a nearby housing project believe that a series of unsolved murders were carried out by a mythical 'Candyman' figure. Legend has it that if you say his name five times into a mirror he will appear, but when Helen does this to disprove the myth it turns out that the Candyman might not be a legend after all.

**Why I Love This Movie**

By the time Candyman came out in 1992, I had been very familiar with Clive Barker for a number of years. I'd seen both of his directorial efforts, 1987's Hellraiser and 1990's much underrated Nightbreed, and loved them both, but it was his short stories, collected in six volumes called the Books of Blood, that had really captivated me.

Barker had a way of, to borrow the title of a series of comic books that were produced based on the Books of Blood, tapping the vein of what really creeped people out in the modern world. His gritty, often extremely graphic stories dealt not with those nasty things that lurked in gothic castles or far off lands, but those that were right there in your backyard. The best of these, and my favourite story from the Books of Blood was a tale called The Forbidden, which explored the idea of urban legends.

Considering the extent to which urban legends are a part of modern life I find it amazing that there haven't been more genre movies based around the premise. The most obvious one of the modest crop is 1998's Urban Legend which went down the teen stalk and slash route, as did the whole Nightmare On Elm Street series, the urban myth element of which was most evident at the beginning of 2003's Freddy vs Jason when Krueger complains that his power has diminished because the children no longer remember him and thus no longer fear him. What I love about Candyman, though, is that writer and director Bernard Rose took all of the important elements from Clive Barker's original story and created a serious, intelligent movie about the power of myth.

To carry off a serious look at this subject, you need a credible actor to shoulder the role, and so Virginia Madsen's character Helen Lyle is a refreshing change from the usual teen heroines that we get served up in our beloved genre, and brings some real gravitas to the movie. It's a testament to how convincingly she embraces this role that I find it very easy to believe that she and her fellow graduate student Bernadette Walsh are intelligent, resourceful young women rather than the usual cannon fodder. Consequently when things start to take a turn for the surreal, her performance is compelling as she finds herself with no control over the increasingly nightmarish situations that she finds herself in.

One of the great strengths of Candyman for me is that although there is an obvious supernatural element at play here, the movie itself is firmly grounded in reality. Rose has interwoven the very real thread of race into the script, and by setting the movie in the housing projects of Cabrini Green, at the time a genuine location in Chicago, and having the villain being a black man terrorising a white woman, he manages to make a valid social comment about the urban myths that build up around such areas.

As Vanessa Williams's character Ann-Marie McCoy points out to Helen and Bernadette, society has already made its mind up that all black people living in the projects are on drugs and involved with gangs, but they never consider that this isn't the whole picture. Anne-Marie is just trying to raise her son right, and hopes to steer him clear of 'the idiots downstairs' who *do* roam around in gangs.

The projects, though, have become no go areas that Bernadette, a black woman herself, states that she won't even *drive* past. This is reinforced by the fact that despite Anne-Marie calling the police after hearing her neighbour Ruthie Jean screaming on the night of her murder, no patrol cars were despatched.

It is within this environment of fear and isolation that urban legends like the Candyman are able to flourish. As Helen discovers in a brutal encounter in a public convenience, the power of the myth enables a local gang leader to adopt the persona of the Candyman in order to rule the estate by fear, his murderous escapades being blamed on the whispered tales.

Thanks to a script of such depth and perception, Rose is able to keep the Candyman himself out of the picture for the whole of the first half, effectively allowing us, the audience, to discover the myth and allow it to grow by word of mouth via many characters who speak of him in hushed and almost reverential tones. As with all well paced and tightly plotted movies, Rose's refusal to reveal his trump card until as late as possible pays off magnificently.

When we do finally meet the Candyman, the restrained but hypnotising power that he exudes on screen can be attributed to genre veteran Tony Todd. He has a certain presence that perfectly conjures up the air of regality that accompanies the Candyman's origin. Daniel Robitaille was a well-educated son of a slave who rose to prominence in 'polite society' as a portrait artist, but happened to fall in love with the wrong woman leading to his brutal murder at the behest of her father.

Todd brings a grace and elegance to the role, which unlike many of the genre killers is not borne of revenge or sadism, but rather of love and the desire to propagate his legend. It becomes apparent in the later stages of the movie that Helen is much more than just some random victim who has foolishly spoken Candyman's name five times into the mirror. The revelation about their relationship, which echoes the final shot of the picture on the Overlook's wall at the conclusion of Stanley Kubrick's 1980 interpretation of The Shining, satisfactorily explains why he didn't slaughter her when she invoked him, as he had done the rest of his victims.

Instead he effective courts her throughout the second half of the movie, but in such a way that he places her in increasingly horrific situations until she really has no choice but to agree to his request to 'be my victim' and join him in mythological posterity.

The interaction and chemistry between Todd and Madsen on screen is of such strength and power that you can almost feel the electricity between them. Thanks to Rose's insistence that Madsen be actually hypnotised during her scenes with Todd she exudes a wonderfully dreamy, almost helpless state in his presence, which helps immensely in selling the idea that they may have been destined to come together from the very start.

The increasingly bizarre situations that Helen finds herself in are skilfully handled by Rose, and manage to keep us as off balance as she is. In one scene she wakes up in a pool of blood, the severed head of a dog nearby, and Anne-Marie attacking her for apparently stealing her baby. At this point we have no idea how we got here from the previous scene, but neither does Helen, and so we are effectively taking her surreal journey with her.

What I love about Candyman as a villain is that he shares many of the same attributes as a couple of my other favourite maniacs, namely Michael Myers and Jason Vorhees. Like them, his actions are very measured and precise, the actions of a man fully in control of what he is doing. He feels no need to jump out and scare his victims or to wise crack like my favourite fedora wearing child killer, but instead speaks in a wonderfully deep and resonant voice that holds your attention in a vice-like grip.

While Jason and Michael have been played by a number of talented actors over the years, Candyman is one of those roles that I just cannot imagine anyone else being able to nail with such conviction as Todd does. He has this in common with another of Clive Barker's creations, Pinhead, who could never, in my eyes, be played by anyone except Doug Bradley. The same goes for Mr Krueger and Robert Englund.

Another of the things that I find so appealing about Candyman, and that draws me back to it again and again is the look of the movie. The graffiti covered walls of the Cabrini Green tower blocks are both beautifully decorative and depressingly oppressive, and the mural of the Candyman on the wall of the apartment where he supposedly resides is simple but extremely effective. The first time we see it, Helen is peering through a hole in the wall, at which point the camera slowly pulls back to reveal that the hole is in fact his mouth in a huge portrait of him.

The murals of his origin, too, are wonderful. Rose pulls a masterstroke by electing not to graphically show Daniel Robitaille's fate (that finally happened in the sequel, Candyman Farewell To The Flesh), but instead having his origin verbally told to Helen, and to the audience, over dinner earlier in the movie and then reprising it through the faded wall paintings that she discovers in the final reel.

The pacing of the movie is near perfect. It's not quite sedate enough to be considered a true slow burner, but Rose unfolds the story in a measured and controlled manner, very effectively building the confusion as to what is happening to Helen's character and the sense of her horrificaly inevitable destiny.

This careful pacing is beautifully underpinned by a sparse score by veteran composer Phillip Glass, consisting only of piano, organ and choral voices. This minimalistic approach gives Candyman an epic feel, and deliberately resists the urge to telegraph the scares and revelations to the audience as many genre scores tend to do.

Candyman, for me, remains the definitive urban legend movie. It is both intelligent and at times brutal and horrific as Candyman goes to whatever lengths are necessary to win back his true love, and is a perfect example of how to make an effective, enjoyable horror movie without having to resort to tired old clichés (though the final moments are deliciously predictable but satisfyingly enjoyable).

**My Favourite Scene**

The first time we actually meet Candyman.

Helen has returned to her car in the university parking garage and we hear a low, baritone voice call her name, almost singing it, in a nod to the main theme's nursery rhyme feel. She stops and turns and we see at the far end of the level a man dressed in a long, regal coat, as though he is going to the opera.

He walks towards her, unhurried, telling her that he has come for her because she was not satisfied with the stories and asks her to 'be my victim'.

This is such a simple reveal, but one that is chilling and extremely effective thanks to Todd's imposing and regal presence on the screen and Madsen's helpless, hypnotic response to him, like a rabbit caught in the headlights of an oncoming car.

**Did You Know That...**

Clive Barker's original short story The Forbidden was set in Liverpool, England, the city he grew up in, and that the legend itself was inspired by a tale that his Grandmother told him when he was four years old of men who lurked in public toilets and cut off the genitals of small boys.

The 'sweets to the sweet' graffiti that Helen finds in Candyman's apartment and in the toilets where a young boy is murdered is derived from a line in William Shakespeare's Hamlet.

Real bees were used for the scene where Tony Todd has them emerge from his mouth. His only protection was a mouth shield to prevent him from swallowing any of them.

If Virginia Madsen had been unavailable for the role of Helen Lyle the part would most likely have gone to Sandra Bullock, an unknown actress at this point.

Cabrini Green was a real housing project in Chicago, and the filmmakers had to effectively pay off the local gangs to ensure that they could film there in safety. This worked out well until the final day of shooting when a bullet was fired into the roof of one of the trucks from the roof of the tower block, at which point the crew quickly packed up and left. Cabrini Green has since been demolished.

Xander Berkeley is probably best known for his role as George Mason in the second season of 24.

# Carrie (1976)

Directed by:   Brian De Palma
Written by:    Lawrence D Cohen (based on the novel
                by Stephen King)
Starring:       Sissy Spacek – Carrie White
                Piper Laurie – Margaret White
                Amy Irving – Susan Snell
                Nancy Allen – Christine Hargensen
                Brenda Buckley – Miss Watson
                P J Soles – Norma Watson
                John Travolta – Billy Nolan

## Synopsis

After being banned from attending the Senior Prom for taunting Carrie White in the showers when she gets her first period, school bully Chris Hargensen plots her revenge. Another of her tormentors, Susan Snell, feels remorse for her actions and takes pity on Carrie, asking her boyfriend Tommy to take her to the Prom.

When the elections for King and Queen are rigged, however, and Carrie is humiliated in front of the whole school she unleashes her unique gift and makes Prom night one that nobody will ever forget.

## Why I Love This Movie

Carrie will forever hold a very special place in my heart, not just because it was the first 'modern' horror movie that I ever saw and the movie that set up my lifelong obsession with all things macabre and horrific, but because it was a finely crafted movie that even today, three decades after it was made, is a textbook example of what a great horror movie should be.

Brian De Palma saw the potential for a kick-ass horror movie in Stephen King's debut novel, which despite his subsequent crowning as the 'King of Horror' was actually more a tale of teenage awakening and the awkward politics of high school than an out and out horror story. Sure, the premise of Carrie White being a telekinetic outsider who is pushed to breaking point, and then reacts with ferocious and bloody vengeance on her tormentors is classic horror fare, but King's real home run with his novel was to nail the feeling of isolation and rejection felt by someone who isn't part of the 'in crowd'.

This was exactly how I, and many others I suspect, felt in my early school years, and the reason why this movie and novel initially hit home with the accuracy of a laser guided missile, and why it continues to be an important movie in my life to this day.

What makes Carrie such a watchable movie, though, is largely down to De Palma's imaginative and original direction. Thanks to the fact that he had several months to visualise and storyboard the movie before he shot a single frame of film, he was able to create a picture that not only flows smoothly from the opening volleyball game to the closing, heart-stopping shot, but is a joy to watch, never once feeling sluggish despite the slow burn nature of the tale.

He employs several techniques that have rarely been used to such great effect since, the most obvious being his use of split screen to devastating effect in the scenes of carnage that ultimately play out in the Bates High School gymnasium, and more unusually the use of a split dioptre lens which allows a single shot to focus on both the foreground and the background simultaneously.

A great example of this is in the scene where Carrie describes Tommy Ross's poem as beautiful. In the background, on the right of the screen, we are focussed on Carrie, her head bowed as she sits lost in the beauty of Tommy's poem, while in the foreground, on the left of the screen, Ross sits with a 'why me' expression on his face as he prepares for the backlash of being the object of the class outcast's attention.

While Carrie could be classed as the first teen horror movie, this is no Final Destination or I Know What You Did Last Summer. The characters in De Palma's movie, thanks to screenwriter Lawrence D Cohen's perceptive interpretation of King's novel, are fully rounded and are given time to breathe and grow on screen into kids that we either love or hate, but ultimately give a damn about.

Sissy Spacek is perfectly cast as Carrie, a girl who thanks to her religiously fanatical mother has been cast as the outsider in her school, and who aches to be accepted by her peers. Her terror as she experiences her first period in the showers and is then cornered by her classmates, who revert frighteningly quickly to the age old pack mentality of turning on the weak member in their group, is heartbreaking. Carrie has effectively been betrayed by her mother, who hasn't prepared her for the onset of womanhood, making her believe instead that it is a sign that she has fallen into sin and must be forced to repent.

Piper Laurie, who returned to the big screen for the first time in sixteen years on the strength of Cohen's script, is chilling as Margaret White. She is a woman driven by her religious beliefs and rendered bitter and twisted after being raped by Carrie's father (in her perception of events), her one and only experience of the evils of intercourse, which produced her daughter who she now believes she must protect from the big bad world. She projects her self loathing onto Carrie in the form of extreme child abuse, hitting her and repeatedly locking her in a small, dark cupboard to pray and consider her sins, her only company in there a bible, a candle and a grotesque effigy of Saint Sebastian impaled by a number of arrows.

Laurie plays this role with real relish. From the first time we see her in the warm, 'normal' confines of the Snell household as she tries to warn Sue's mother of the dangers of youthful corruption, to her final act of attempted infanticide, we know that this woman is possessed with a religious fervour that knows no logic or rationality. Such is her single mindedness that when Carrie is getting ready for the Prom in a handmade light pink dress, she takes one look at it and declares 'Red, I might have known it would be red', clearly transfixed on Carrie's sinful menstruation.

When Tommy Ross invites Carrie to the Prom, she is terrified that her only daughter will fall further into sin and be lost to the Devil, and does her best to undermine her new found confidence and hope that she can be accepted by her peers.

In compete contrast, Betty Buckley's Miss Collins shows great sympathy to Carrie's reaction to her period and the subsequent torment she receives from her classmates, encouraging her to accept Tommy's invitation to the Prom and to integrate herself with her peers. She is the mother figure that Margaret White, lost in her religious mania, can never be.

Amy Irving, as Sue Snell, makes us believe that her grand gesture of getting her boyfriend to take Carrie to the Prom as her penance for joining in the locker room torment is genuine, and William Katt, as Tommy Ross, convinces us that not only are his intentions in carrying out this gesture equally genuine (after an initial reluctance to do so), but that he really is having a good time with Carrie at the dance, finally seeing her for the beautiful and interesting person that she is.

This interaction between the two of them, as he makes her seemingly impossible dream of integrating with and being accepted by her peers and thus being 'normal' come true, and then as the ultimate fairytale ending is seemingly bestowed upon her when they are crowned King and Queen of the Prom, serve to make the final denouement all the more heartbreaking.

De Palma's slow and deliberate pacing for the first two acts of the movie works perfectly in making this date between the most popular guy and the most unpopular girl in school utterly believable. Despite the final reel carnage this is almost the archetypal love story, with the ugly duckling becoming a swan and marrying her Prince Charming, but of course with every good fairytale there are always the villains lurking in the background.

Enraged at being banned from the Prom after refusing to accept her punishment for tormenting Carrie in the locker room, Chris Hargensen, played with devastating vitriol by Nancy Allen, enlists the help of her morally bankrupt boyfriend Billy Nolan, John Travolta in his first movie role, to exact her revenge on Carrie and make sure she has a night to remember for all the wrong reasons.

This forms the pivotal point of the final act, and De Palma delivers one of the finest sequences that I've seen to this day in a horror movie as their dastardly plan is put into action and seals everybodies fate. Using slow motion for several minutes, De Palma creates an incredible tension as we watch the actions of the main characters intersect in an almost balletic manner as everybody unwittingly reacts in the wrong way and everything goes to hell. Once this happens, Spacek gives the performance of her life, which even now scares me as she stands first in shocked disbelief, and then cold, calculated rage as she exacts her revenge.

Along with The Omen, Carrie is one of the few horror movies from the 1970s that keeps me coming back time and again. De Palma hit a home run with this picture, and it always surpasses my expectations every time I watch it. In retrospect, I couldn't have chosen a better movie to lose my modern horror movie virginity to.

## My Favourite Scene

The White house has been razed to the ground, and a real estate board knocked into the ground in front of it. Someone has daubed 'Carrie White burns in hell' on it in red paint, a crude arrow pointing downwards.

Sue Snell, the girl who let her boyfriend take Carrie to the Prom walks nervously up to the plot, a bunch of flowers in her hand. She reaches the sign and kneels to place the flowers there, her face awash with guilt.

As the camera zooms in on the flowers, a bloodied hand suddenly thrusts its way through the earth and grabs her wrist, prompting heart attacks in all but the most resilient of movie goers. At this point, my eight-year-old backside cleared the sofa by a good three inches as this celluloid moment burned itself into my mind forever.

Even after seeing this scene numerous times over the years, and being fully aware of what is coming, I *still* jump several inches off the sofa when that hand appears.

**Did You Know That...**

P J Soles reunited with John Travolta the same year (1976) for The Boy In The Plastic Bubble, a TV movie about a boy who is born with a deficient immune system.

Director Brian De Palma held joint auditions for Carrie with a fellow director called George Lucas who was casting for some low budget space opera called Star Wars.

At these auditions, William Katt (Tommy Ross) read for the part of Han Solo and Amy Irving (Susan Snell) read for the part of Princess Leia.

Carrie was turned into a musical that debuted in Stratford, England before moving to Broadway and closing after just five performances.

The high school in the movie is called Bates High in homage to Psycho's cross-dressing mama's boy Norman Bates.

The hand that shoots up through the ground at the end does actually belong to Sissy Spacek, who insisted on doing all her own 'hand work'.

# Creep (2004)

Directed by:    Christopher Smith
Written by:     Christopher Smith
Starring:       Franke Potente – Kate
                Vas Blackwood – George
                Ken Campbell – Arthur
                Jeremy Sheffield – Guy
                Kelly Scott – Mandy
                Sean Harris - Craig

## Synopsis

After falling asleep on a platform in the London Underground system, a young woman wakes up to find herself locked in. Searching for a way out it becomes apparent that she is not alone, and finds herself fending off an attack from an amorous colleague who has followed her down there from a party they had both attended earlier.

However, after he is suddenly attacked and dragged off into the darkness it becomes apparent that he is the least of her worries down there in the tunnels.

## Why I Love This Movie

I've always had a thing for terror in tunnels, whether it was the borderline terrible 1984 movie C.H.U.D. about the titular cannibalistic humanoid underground dwellers in New York, or the far superior novel Relic by Lincoln Preston, on which the entertaining but decidedly average 1997 movie of the same name was based, and its worthy sequel Reliquary. The daddy of them all for me, though, was the novel by Terrance Dicks based on the six-part Dr Who story The Web Of Fear that was originally broadcast in 1968.

Thanks to the British Broadcasting Company's policy of regularly wiping videotapes and reusing them (who knew there would be a market for low budget television series in the future, eh?), all but the first episode of this story has been lost forever, but as a young boy I devoured Dr Who books like nobody's business and this was one of my favourite stories. The idea of killer Yeti wandering through the tunnels of the London Underground, which at the time I had no experience of, was strangely appealing, so when nearly a quarter of a century later I read that Christopher Smith's upcoming movie Creep was to be set in those very same tunnels, that alone gave me cause to become excited about it.

On top of that, however, was the fact that in the intervening years I had visited London numerous times and have lived there since 2000, so the prospect of seeing a British horror movie not only based in the tunnels that I travel through on a regular basis, but also actually shot on location in them, pushed my anticipation of this movie into overdrive.

For those of you reading this with knowledge of any of the world's underground systems, be they the New York Subway, the Metro in Paris or any of the numerous others located around the globe, there will be no need to conjure up the feeling of being deep beneath street level late at night once the platforms become empty and silent, feeling the stillness of the air and the eerie quiet that hangs thickly around you in between the arrival of the trains. When busy, these stations and tunnels are alive and feel safe, but if you find yourself down there alone for any length of time the icy tendrils of fear begin to creep slowly down the back of your neck.

It is this feeling that Smith plays upon once Famke Potente's character Kate finds herself in such a situation after having dozed off waiting for a late train. Having already been shown in the long prologue that there is something rather unpleasant and not in the least bit friendly down there in the tunnels, shot largely with flashlight beams as the sole light source, I found myself genuinely concerned for Kate as she awakes to find herself locked in and alone, or so she believes.

Smith expertly prowls the tiled circular corridors of Charing Cross Station, making full use of his hand held camera to create a claustrophobic prison for Kate as she quickly realises her predicament, and then throws in a very human threat in the form of her unwelcome stalker colleague. In much the same way that the Blair Witch Project would have been equally as scary, if not more so, without the supernatural element, the danger that Kate finds herself in from this very real situation is sinister enough, but he then introduces a greater, and cleverly unseen threat that initially seems to save her from one terrible scenario only to put her at the mercy of a more dangerous assailant.

Creep is very much a movie of two halves, the first being an almost formulaic but enjoyable retread of many a stalk and slash movie as we are introduced to several characters who are subsequently bumped off, but then Smith pulls one of the great movie villain reveals, rivalled only by a coincidentally similar one in Neil Marshall's The Descent, released the same year, and suddenly the movie jumps tracks and we find ourselves with a monster, of sorts, that I found myself actually empathising with to a degree.

Much of the credit for this goes to Sean Harris, who plays the eponymous Creep, stalking the screen with a confident yet vulnerable and almost innocent presence. Physically resembling a cross between how you would imagine Ari Lehman's Jason Vorhees from 1980's Friday The 13th would look all grown up, and Bub, the charismatic zombie from George A Romero's 1986 Day Of The Dead, the Creep is an emaciated and pathetic figure.

Thanks to a reasonably convincing back story, much of which is implied, crediting the audience with some intelligence in being able to piece the clues and information together for themselves, the Creep is given something of an air of the tragic victim, akin to the Phantom of the Opera, without diluting the fact that you really do not want to meet him in a dark tunnel, or anywhere else for that matter.

I personally love it when there is a certain vulnerability to a movie monster. While the Freddys, Jasons and Michaels of this world are fun to watch as they relentlessly pursue their victims, it is the Leatherfaces, Normans and Creeps of this world, who you feel are as much victims themselves in many ways as the people they prey upon, that garner my sympathies.

The Creep, or Craig as we discover his name is through an effective scene in which Kate and another character (whose identity I won't reveal for fear of spoiling it for those of you who haven't seen this movie yet) find themselves in a dank and run down nursery-cum-laboratory, isn't wilfully evil or deliberately sadistic, but is instead just following the twisted but logical path (well, logical to him anyway) that his upbringing has taught him is 'normal'. They discover four cribs, surrounded by all manner of children's toys, shelves full of bottled foetuses, and faded framed photographs that hint at what once went on down in this disused tube station.

It's exactly this sort of set that I really love in movies. It puts you instantly at unease, and whether deep underground as it is here, or in the backwoods *á la* Wrong Turn or The Texas Chain Saw Massacre, or in the government installations of Resident Evil or Day Of The Dead, it hints at terrible things that the imagination fills in the blanks in for far more effectively than any amount of exposition.

Creep also delivers in the gore stakes, and I applaud Smith for standing proud among the ranks of the new breed of directors, including Eli Roth, Neil Marshall, Rob Zombie and Alexandre Aja, who aren't afraid to be true to the roots of our beloved genre, rather than bow down at the altar of the teen friendly, sanitised and compromised fare that much of the last decade's offerings turned out to be. The British Board of Film Classification even went as far as to put warnings on the posters and DVD box for Creep that it contained scenes of 'strong bloody violence', the promise of which was delivered in spades, particularly during one scene involving Craig's amateur attempts at a surgical procedure, more of which later.

The movie isn't without its flaws, though. Craig aside, none of the characters are especially engaging, particularly Kate who I never really found myself warming to. Early on in the movie she is asked if she can spare some change by a homeless person sitting near the cash machine that she is using to which she replies "This machine dispenses notes. If you're looking for change why don't you hang around a phone box?"

Then later while Jimmy, one half of a homeless junkie couple living in the tube station, is telling her about himself and his partner Mandy she turns to him and says "OK, listen sweetie. I don't mean to be rude but I don't care about your lifetime story right now." This didn't exactly endear Kate to me, and so I found my sympathies were actually lying more with Craig than with her. To be fair, though, writer and director Smith stated that this was one of his objectives, to make the audience empathise with the Creep, so perhaps the apathy I felt as to whether the other subterranean supporting cast members lived or died was intentional after all.

However, this doesn't detract from the overall enjoyment of the movie, and clocking in at a decidedly old school running time of 82 minutes it doesn't have time to outstay its welcome. Creep, like several other movies in this book, will never be considered a genre classic nor essential viewing in the eyes of many horror fans, but for me the tragic nature of Craig's existence and the physical location of the movie, set and filmed on platforms and corridors that I have actually physically stood on and walked through, make this a film that I can happily watch again and again.

Creep is, to use the inevitable pun, very creepy in places thanks to Smith making full use of the claustrophobic Victorian tunnels and stations, and delivers some good solid Saturday Night Fright Flick scares. Older genre fans will invariably compare it, and rightly so, to the 1972 flick Death Line which was also set in the London Underground system and featured another cannibalistic humanoid underground dweller, but Creep brings plenty of its own character to these familiar locations.

In lieu of the fact that I will never get the chance to see Dr Who's Yeti prowling these tunnels, Creep will no doubt remain my London Underground terror flick of choice for years to come.

## My Favourite Scene

Having been left for dead by Kate and George, the Creep enters the room where Mandy is held in a surgeon's chair, her feet in birthing stirrups. Acting out a procedure that he remembers the man we assume to be his father carrying out in the past, he adjusts the broken operating room light and then cradles Mandy's head in his hands, as if comforting her, while she pleads for her life.

Craig turns on a tap from which no water emerges and 'washes' his hands. He dresses himself in a surgeon's smock and clumsily pulls on some ill-fitting, ancient latex gloves before walking over to Mandy and using a non-functioning gas mask administers non-existent anaesthetic to her before he begins his work.

This scene is filled with a certain sadness and pathos up to this point, as we see the child within Craig desperately trying to emulate his father, but once he picks up his two foot long serrated blade, we are into classic stomach churning horror territory. Employing the maxim that what you don't see is worse then what you do, we see a close up of Craig's emotionless face as he works the blade, blood splattering onto his gaunt skin.

A very intense and disturbing scene that, in common with Tobe Hooper's 1974 classic The Texas Chain Saw Massacre, has you thinking that you have seen much more than you actually have, and one that will stay with you long after the credits have rolled.

**Did You Know That...**

Jeremy Sheffield was a regular in BBC TV's hospital drama series Holby City, playing Doctor Alex Adams. He also appeared in the music video for Natalie Imbruglia's hit single Torn.

The original poster for the movie, which portrayed a bloody hand sliding down the window of a tube train, was banned by London Underground for being in bad taste, despite the fact that they had permitted Smith to film in several disused stations. The ban was lifted in time for the DVD release but not for the theatrical run.

Before deciding on Creep, other titles that were considered included 'Runt', Here Kitty Kitty', 'One Track Mind' and 'Piccadilly Nightmare'.

# Dawn of the Dead (1978)

Directed by:   George A Romero
Written by:    George A Romero
Starring:      David Emge – Stephen Andrews
               Ken Foree – Peter Washington
               Scott H Reiniger – Roger DeMarco
               Gaylen Ross – Francine Parker

**Synopsis**

The dead are rising and feeding on the living! As zombies overrun the cities, four people escape in a helicopter to an out of town mall where they seem to have everything they need to live comfortably.

However, it soon becomes apparent that the greatest threat to their safety isn't from the zombies themselves, but from a biker gang who have also set their sights on the mall.

**Why I Love This Movie**

I have a passion for zombie movies, regardless of whether the undead are of the classic slow shuffling variety or the recent sprinters, but in common with many genre fans, whenever the word 'zombie' is mentioned there is one film that springs immediately to mind. George A Romero's 1978 classic Dawn Of The Dead.

This is, quite simply, the quintessential zombie movie, combining action, an intelligent and thought provoking script, four appealing and likeable lead characters, and all the gore that you could hope for in your wildest and most disturbing dreams.

Dawn Of The Dead was the first modern zombie movie that I can remember seeing, and ingrained itself on my subconscious in much the same way that my first kiss did, though with a lot more blood and violence (the movie, that is, not the kiss.)

In common with Fulci's 1979 Zombie Flesh Eaters, Romero throws us in at the deep end, opening the movie in the middle of a television station going into meltdown as the chaos of the overwhelming zombie outbreak brings the county to a standstill.

As in all of Romero's zombie movies, we are given no explicit explanation as to why the dead are rising, and none is needed. All we need to know is that civilisation as we know it is on an express train to hell (where by all accounts there are no vacancies), and that we are along for the ride.

What sets Dawn apart from other zombie movies are the wonderfully three-dimensional main characters. Peter, Roger, Fran and Stephen are not just cannon fodder waiting to be ticked off the death list, they are believable human beings who it's hard not to care about and worry for their well-being.

The four leads play off each other magnificently. Peter is the battle hardened and rational trooper who juxtaposes his impulsive and overconfident colleague Roger, while Stephen tries and repeatedly fails to live up to their macho and self-assured behaviour. Fran is the real revelation, however, undergoing a shift from meek victim to self-assured survivor a good year before Ellen Ripley was lauded for a similar transformation.

The chemistry between the actors completely sells the reality of the situation that they find themselves in, the relationship between the two troopers being especially believable, helped undoubtedly by Foree and Reiniger's close friendship in real life.

The real stars of the movie, though, are the zombies. Never before, or since, have so many of the undead appeared on screen, culminating in nearly five hundred for the final showdown with the army of bikers.

In my opinion, Tom Savini's work on this movie has never been bettered in terms of imagination and originality. Though destined to be much imitated over the years, Dawn was the first flick to offer up zombie kids being machine-gunned, redneck zombie lynching parties, and the unforgettable sight of a zombie's head being removed by a helicopter rotor (though sadly, and inexplicably, this doesn't appear in Dario Argento's European Cut of the movie).

Like his fellow pioneer Rob Bottin, whose work on John Carpenter's 1982 remake of The Thing still stands for me as the greatest example of special effects ever committed to celluloid, Savini didn't have CGI to play with back then, and so every shot, every effect had to be done 'for real', and is so much more effective as a result.

Though in this age of endless DVD behind the scenes features and internet forums we now know exactly how all of these tricks were performed, it takes none of the magic away from their execution onscreen. The myriad of gunshot wounds, exploding heads, bites, and the geysers of blood that accompany them still have me grinning in delight whenever I watch Dawn.

It's not all about the gore, though. Romero's not so subtle commentary on the fact that redneck America will turn just about anything into a beer drinking shooting party is just one of the social observations that I love about Dawn. Romero also places the first encounter we have with the 'enemy' in a housing project where the zombies are African American, a theme carried onwards in Bernard Rose's 1992 Candyman which also commented on society's stereotyped and incorrect perception that all black people are dangerous, crack addicts, gangbangers, or all three.

Coming from any other filmmaker these observations, along with the subtle comments such as Peter replying "some brothers" when he is asked if he has lost anyone, might appear crass or even inappropriate, but Romero has the credentials to back them up. Having cast Dwayne Jones as the lead in his 1968 classic Night Of The Living Dead back when lead roles for African

American actors were very few and far between, he accidentally set a precedent for casting the best actor for a role regardless of social convention.

The most accurate observation Romero makes, however, is of the consumer. When Fran asks, "What are they doing? Why do they come here?" Stephen replies "Memory of what they used to do. This was an important place in their lives." This is a sentiment that causes me to think of this movie almost every time I'm in a crowded shopping centre, but particularly in the run up to Christmas, as I watch the hundreds of people shuffle from shop to shop with a singular purpose, to consume.

Another reminder that the undead are not so very different to the average shopper comes when Stephen observes that "They're after us. They know we're still in here." To which Peter astutely replies, "They're after the place. They don't know why, they just remember. Remember that they want to be in here."

Fran asks him, "What the hell are they?" and he tells her, "They're us, that's all." Ken Foree then delivers what is one of my favourite lines of dialogue of all time, and one that has become as ingrained in society as any of the various Star Wars catchphrases over the years, "When there's no more room in hell, the dead will walk the earth."

Romero also makes some poignant and valid comments on the human condition. When they come across a dozen or so zombies contained in the basement of a building, Roger asks Peter, "Why do these people keep them in here?" to which Peter replies, "Because they still believe there's respect in dying."

As a video gamer, I will be forever indebted to Dawn for inspiring, among others, the Resident Evil series. Romero doesn't merely give us a mindless movie where the protagonists just run from zombies and shoot them on a regular basis. Instead he shows them devising intelligent solutions to the situations that they find themselves in.

To prevent the zombies from finding their 'safe' rooms, they build a false wall to hide the entrance, and then access it only via the air ducts that run over the top of the stores. To keep the mall free of zombies they block the four main entrances with trucks and lock the doors. Devastatingly simple ideas, but they give the main characters a real sense of intelligence and resourcefulness, and thus depth.

The great irony of Dawn, though, is that at the end of the movie, despite all the hard work they have put in to make themselves safe, it is human intervention in the form of a biker gang that ultimately destroys their refuge and puts them right back where they started.

Though a bleak movie in terms of theme, I love that Romero has injected a pitch-black sense of humour into it that really works alongside the more weighty concepts and situations. The sight of zombies struggling up and down escalators, or trying to keep their balance on the ice rink, all set to the most ridiculously cheesy muzak ever recorded, always brings a smile to my face.

There is even a pie fight, which as absurd as it sounds actually works in the context of the movie. Thanks to Romero making us believe that the biker gang that invade the mall aren't the least bit threatened or frightened by the zombies, it's not a great stretch to accept them pushing custard pies in their faces and spraying them with soda siphons.

Dawn Of The Dead, for me, has everything that the perfect zombie movie, and indeed horror movie, could possibly need. It rattles along at a cracking pace, with never a dull moment even when the action occasionally slows down to focus on the human stories of the four main characters. It has action, humour and enough blood and body parts to satisfy even the most ardent gorehound.

What I really love about Dawn, though, is that despite the fact the clothes they are wearing have long since been convicted of crimes against fashion, Romero's social commentary still stands up today.

I've lost count of the number of times that I've seen this movie in its various editions, but I can confidently say that I'll be watching it on a regular basis until the day I shuffle off this mortal coil, and maybe even after that if there's no more room in hell when I get there.

## My Favourite Scene

There are so many great scenes in Dawn, but the one that really stands out for me is the final few minutes of the movie.

Peter has decided, much to Fran's horror, that he doesn't want to leave with her, that he's seen enough death and is ready to check himself out.

As he waits alone, with a small pistol to do the job, he suddenly has a change of heart and fights his way through the hordes of zombies that are now surrounding him.

On the roof, Fran has seen zombies coming up through the opening and, assuming that Peter is dead, is about to lift off when he appears, kicks his way through the undead on the roof and throws himself into the back seat of the helicopter.

Though the movie still ends on a bleak note, with Fran and Peter flying off with only a little fuel and no idea of where they can go, that spark of hope and human resistance that grabs hold of Peter has me cheering for him every time.

## Did You Know That...

Ken Foree and Scott Reiniger both had cameos in Zack Snyder's 2004 remake of Dawn Of The Dead, and Gaylen Ross was immortalised by having a store in the new mall named after her.

The original scripted ending had Fran giving up and taking her own life by pushing her head up into the helicopter's rotors, but this was deemed to be too bleak and was never shot.

Tom Savini's niece and nephew, Donna and Mike, played the two zombie children that Peter encounters at the airfield. They are also the only zombies in the entire movie who run, effectively putting a hole in the argument that Romero's zombies never ran.

Real life members of the local chapter of the Pagans Motor-cycle Club were cast as the biker gang.

There are three versions of the movie. The original 127-minute US theatrical version, an extended 139-minute cut, and a 118-minute European version edited by Dario Argento. For the record I favour the extended cut.

# The Descent (2005)

Directed by:   Neil Marshall
Written by:   Neil Marshall
Starring:      Shauna MacDonald – Sarah
                Natalie Mendoza – Juno
                Alex Reid – Beth
                Saskia Mulder – Rebecca
                MyAnna Buring – Sam
                Nora-Jane Noone - Holly

## Synopsis

Six female friends go on a caving expedition, but when they become trapped after a cave-in they discover that they are not alone.

## Why I Love This Movie

Neil Marshall first appeared on my radar with his debut feature, 2002's Dog Soldiers, which put an innovative spin on the werewolf movie and managed to be both gory and intelligent at the same time. I remember coming away from this movie feeling very satisfied and also very proud, because along with Danny Boyle's 28 Days Later, also released in 2002, we at last had a couple of British horror movies that we could be hold up as being every bit as good as, if not better, than those being produced across the pond.

When I began reading about his upcoming sophomore movie, The Descent, I therefore began to get excited at the prospect of another homegrown gem, and Marshall didn't disappoint me. The Descent ranks up among my favourite horror movie experiences in a cinema, and loses none of its impact on the small screen.

In the first five minutes alone Marshall manages to achieve what many other directors can only dream of being capable of. He expertly and effortlessly sets up the friendships between the main characters (all of whom are female), including an implied affair between one of the girls and another's husband, which to his credit he telegraphs to us, the audience, through the subtle way in which the two adulterous characters interact rather than by spoon feeding us as so often tends to be the norm.

To set up these friendships as being believable in the pre-title sequence would have been an achievement in itself, which justifies Marshall's insistence on investing time in finding exactly the right women for the role, but we also get one of the most horrific car accidents that I've ever seen on screen. The immediate aftermath of the crash had me caring about these women from the outset, a gambit that pays off superbly as the movie progresses and the tension and terror begin to build.

As Sarah and her husband are talking while they drive along a wooded road, we can see an approaching vehicle through the windscreen. Initially it appears to be passing on the other side of the road but then there is the terrible realisation that it is going to hit their car, and it does so, but not with the bombast and over the top drama that so many movie car crashes exhibit. Instead we just get a dull thud, as would be the case in real life, followed by a quick and bloody sequence of poles being slammed through Sarah's husband and into the back seat where her daughter is sitting.

The crash is all over in the blink of an eye but the shock of the impact is so powerful that it lingers long after the scene, and well beyond the end of the movie.

The story picks up a year later as the girls reunite for a caving expedition, with scenery that is nothing short of breathtaking, and which acts as the perfect juxtaposition to the cramped, claustrophobic caves that make up the remainder of the movie.

Marshall shows us huge expanses of lush green forests, rushing us through them at high speed alongside the girls' vehicles and then flying high above them, tracking the trucks as they wind their way through the dense trees in shots reminiscent of the opening of Stanley Kubrick's 1980 interpretation of Stephen King's The Shining or the final moments of the original theatrical cut of Ridley Scott's 1982 masterpiece Blade Runner. (The footage used for this was made up of outtakes from Kubrick's movie.)

Just prior to this, scenes of the girls spending what proves to be their last night together in an old log cabin are wonderful, perfectly capturing the feel of a slumber party. Marshall astutely captures Sarah's occasional twinges of pain caused by innocent stray comments, particularly in one devastatingly wounded look as Holly declares that when she's older she wants to have lots of babies.

The Descent really kicks off though, in every sense of the word, once the girls arrive at the cave itself. As they lower themselves into the deep opening amid cinematic shards of sunlight and fine watery mists that put Tomb Raider to shame, there is a real sense that they are leaving the safety of the light and, well, descending into darkness.

Thanks to Marshall's decision to light the interior of the caves using only natural sources, such as flames or flares, the tunnels and caverns take on a life of their own and look absolutely stunning. The feelings of claustrophobia and confinement that this conjured up in the dark confines of the cinema where I first saw the movie were unsettling, and worked even better when watching it again in the much smaller space of my living room.

I suffer ever so slightly from claustrophobia myself, so watching the girls squeeze into tight gaps in the rocks and struggle through impossibly small tunnels in near darkness had the hairs on the back of my neck standing on end and my palms feeling slightly clammy. Consequently when Sarah becomes stuck fast in one of these tiny spaces and is pulled free just as the tunnel behind her caves in I found myself holding my breath, my heart racing.

At this point Marshall cranks up the tension between the women as it becomes apparent that Juno has deceived them, by bringing them to an uncharted cave system, and thus rendering the flight plan that they had registered with the mountain rescue people useless as nobody knows where they actually are. This added element of conflict and division within the group works beautifully as it begins to fragment even before the creatures show up.

Marshall adds vertigo to the tension as the girls come across a seemingly impassable chasm that appears to go on forever and are forced to find a way across it. This is one of my favourite scenes in the movie, drawn out just long enough to set your nerves on edge as one of the girls slowly and uncertainly negotiates her way across to the other side, and then as the others follow her lead. This being a horror movie you just *know* that something is going to go wrong, and of course it does, but I won't spoil that for you here.

Hot on the heels of this we get our first really nasty, grimace-inducing scene. It is a testament to Marshall that despite the fact that we've made it to the half way point of the movie and have seen no creatures and no gore, save for the brief car crash scene at the top of the movie, I found myself on the edge of my seat and caring about the fate of the girls.

The real trick of a horror movie for me is to make the audience either flinch or wince, and I did both as one of the girls suddenly takes a fall and breaks her leg, necessitating a teeth-clenching scene in which her exposed shin bone is popped back into place, along with excruciatingly wet sound effects, and bound in a splint. The combination of sound and superb makeup appliances here make this a deliciously uncomfortable scene to watch, a trick Marshall repeats later in the movie as another of the girls is dragged away, her fingernails shearing off as she tries to grab at the rocks to save herself.

And so to the creatures, who finally make an appearance at the half way mark in the movie. There have been some great monster reveals over the years, and with The Descent Marshall can add his name to the list. We are initial lulled into a false sense of calm during this pivotal, and my favourite, scene, as Sarah slowly uses the infra-red capabilities of Holly's video camera to pan around a cave strewn with what appear to be animal bones, before we are given a subtle but extremely effective look at one of the crawlers (to give them their official name as it appears in the credits).

So effective is this reveal that it takes both Sarah and the audience a moment to process what they are seeing before realisation sets in, and all hell breaks loose. Coincidentally, Christopher Smith's Creep, released the same year, used a broadly similar and equally effective reveal of his creature.

Though there are few confrontation scenes in The Descent, when they do happen Marshall is unafraid to tap into his horror roots and makes them ferocious and bloody, and all the more frightening and effective thanks to the sparse lighting. The attention to character and the establishing of the girls personalities really pays off once the creatures show up, as I found myself really rooting for them, as opposed to merely ticking them off the victim list as is so often the case in horror movies.

In the crawlers, Marshall has created a plausible and truly terrifying danger to the girls, but one with an Achilles heel that once they figure it out, results in some wonderful cat and mouse set pieces, including a close encounter that reminded me of the infirmary scene in David Fincher's underrated 1992 Alien3 where Ripley comes face to face with the alien.

Marshall throws in another homage towards the end of the movie (and I love it when directors do this) by having Juno briefly tangle with one of the crawlers underwater, echoing the zombie versus shark melee in Lucio Fulci's 1979 Zombie Flesh Eaters.

Once the crawlers have shown up, Marshall expertly manages to keep the tension cranked up to eleven for the remainder of the movie. Even on the many repeat viewings that I've given The Descent, every time I see it I'm on the edge of my seat. It's not only the tension that Marshall cranks up, though, but also the interplay between the girls. Two of the characters are put through separate situations that ultimately shape their fate, and set up a surprising, but not illogical confrontation that brings an intelligent and brutal closure to their relationship.

In this final reel one of the characters undergoes an Ellen Ripley-esque transformation, evolving into a killer through necessity in a scene that genuinely tugs at the emotions, and the other shows her true colours, which puts the two girls on a collision course. It's this sort of intelligent character development and subtext that, for me, lifts The Descent into the arena of the classic horror movie, and I applaud Marshall for giving the audience enough credit to figure everything out for themselves.

The final thing I love about The Descent is that after ninety minutes of tension, horror and gallons of gore, Marshall doesn't feel the need to give us a nice fluffy ending. In fact the ending is extremely ambiguous, fuelled by Sarah's dream sequences throughout the movie, and leaves me satisfied every time. Sadly, the ending was trimmed for American audiences to give them more closure, and in doing so insults their intelligence by implying that they can't deal with such an ambiguous ending.

In my opinion the movie loses a lot of its impact because of this, but the original ending is on the DVD so you those of you reading this in the United States can make your own mind up.

The Descent is an essential addition to any horror movie collection, and a perfect Saturday Night Fright Flick.

## My Favourite Scene

The initial reveal of the creatures.

The girls find themselves in a dark cavern and Sarah decides to see what is in there using the infrared viewing capability on Holly's video camera. She pans around the chamber and discovers that they are standing among what appear to be hundreds of animal bones. As she pans across each of the girl's faces we suddenly notice one of the creatures in the background, at which point all hell breaks loose.

## Did You Know That...

The look of the creatures was kept a secret from the cast until they were filming the first scene in which they appeared. When they were finally revealed the girls were genuinely freaked out and ran off the set, screaming and laughing.

While doing a film production degree at Newcastle Polytechnic, Marshall handed in a bogus treatment for his coursework and instead secretly filmed a twenty-minute zombie movie called Brain Death. Although it technically broke the rules of his course, because it got such a great reaction when screened his tutors were forced to award him a 2-2 degree.

# Friday 13<sup>th</sup> Part VI : Jason Lives (1986)

Directed by:     Tom McLoughlin
Written by:      Tom McLoughlin
Starring:        Thom Matthews – Tommy Jarvis
                 Jennifer Cooke – Megan Garris
                 David Kagen – Sheriff Michael Garris
                 Kerry Noonan – Paula
                 Renee Jones – Sissy Baker
                 Tom Fridley – Cort
                 C J Graham – Jason Vorhees

## Synopsis

After killing Jason Vorhees several years previously at Camp Crystal Lake, an older Tommy Jarvis absconds from the mental institution where he has been residing and drives out to his grave to convince himself once and for all that Jason is really dead.

After digging him up and confirming that the maniac's body is in fact there, he is about to bring closure to his quest by cremating Jason's body when a freak lightning strike resurrects him. Tommy then has to try and convince the local Sheriff that Jason is back from the dead before the carnage starts all over again.

## Why I Love This Movie

Although I whole-heartedly agree with the old adage that the original of anything is usually the best, including the first Friday

13<sup>th</sup> movie (which I adore), it is Part VI : Jason Lives that I find myself returning to time and again.

I was sixteen when the movie came out in 1986 and had just reached the point where I was able to bluff my way into cinemas to see horror movies. I had also recently become a regular Fangoria reader, and was aware that not only was there a new Friday 13<sup>th</sup> movie on the way, but that the chances were good it would get a cinema release thanks to the recent success of other horror flicks like the first two Elm Street movies and Fright Night. The fact that Alice Cooper was doing the music for it, contributing the theme tune He's Back (The Man Behind The Mask) as well as a couple of his classic tunes, was the icing on the cake for this teenage rock fan.

Jason Lives therefore had the distinction of being the first Friday 13<sup>th</sup> movie that I actually saw on the big screen, playing as part of a double bill at the now demolished ABC cinema in my hometown of Nottingham with the very much underrated April Fool's Day, a reasonably entertaining teen slasher update of Agatha Christie's classic Ten Little Indians.

I'd seen parts one, three and four prior to this, and so was more than familiar with Jason, but as writer and director Tom McLoughlin had promised in Fango, this was to be a very different Jason to the one that we knew and loved. In terms of the fans, he had a lot of work to do in order to get rid of the nasty taste that the revelation about Part V's Jason had left in their mouths, but McLoughlin came through magnificently, although not without controversy of his own.

While the fans were clamouring for a return to the serious stalk and slash of earlier entries, McLoughlin elected to take a slightly different route by injecting some humour into the proceedings. One of the things that I love about Part VI is that while its humour is nowhere near as blatant as straight up horror comedies like 1985's superb Return Of The Living Dead, this is a movie that definitely doesn't take itself too seriously. Part VI plays like a love letter to the fans, retaining all of the important elements from the series, and crucially never making Jason look in any way camp (pun fully intended) or ridiculous, but at the same time tipping knowing winks to the audience that it acknowledges the absurdity of certain characters and situations.

A classic example of this is where a couple come across Jason standing in the middle of the road, brandishing a long metal railing. The woman slams on the brakes and strongly suggests that they turn around because she has 'seen enough horror movies to know that any weirdo wearing a mask is never friendly'. Another nod comes later when the old cemetery caretaker comes across Jason's open grave, then turns to the camera and asks 'Why'd they have to go and dig up Jason? Some folks have got a weird idea of entertainment'.

Despite the nods to the audience, however, Thom Matthews maintains the integrity of the core story by never having Tommy Jarvis break from his determined mission to first get the Sheriff to believe that, thanks to him, Jason has returned, and then when his pleas fall on deaf ears to go after Jason himself.

Though Kane Hodder is generally considered to be the fans' favourite incarnation of Jason, and was the only actor to reprise the role, wearing the trademark hockey mask from 1988's Part VII : The New Blood through to 2001's Jason X, former nightclub owner C J Graham puts in a great performance in Part VI.

The actual look of Jason is a revelation compared to the men in jumpsuits who had come before him. Our first glimpse of him is as a rotting, maggot infested corpse lying in his grave, but once he's back up and around, Graham gives him a real air of menace and threat, using his imposing body language to convince us that this new zombie Jason (though there are those who consider Jason to have been undead from the very first film) is much more dangerous than previous incarnations.

Graham brings a powerful presence to the screen, nailing the slow, deliberate walk that makes Mr Vorhees (and indeed my favourite masked maniac Mr Myers) such a frightening proposition. He even throws in a very subtle nod, literally, to Michael when Jason comes across a motor home rocking under the exertions of the teens having sex inside and he tilts his head ever so slightly to the right.

It is this motor home that provides one of the greatest set pieces in the whole Friday series for me, as Jason takes out the two teens and causes it to overturn and burst into flames. As the vehicle burns, there is a beautiful shot of Jason standing on its roof that is worthy of American Cinematographer magazine.

The rest of the movie looks great as well, from the moody, rain lashed opening scenes in the cemetery where Tommy unwittingly resurrects his nemesis, to the shots of the darkened woods with white fog drifting lazily among the trees, to the ring of fire on the water at the end where Tommy has his final showdown with Jason.

The body count, too, is suitably high, thanks to the script not worrying too much about depth of plot and instead setting up set piece after set piece to bring the final total to a respectable eighteen. The only tragedy is that thanks to the MPAA being stricter back in 1986 than they seem to be these days, many of the kills are actually carried out off screen or out of frame, but this doesn't detract too much from the movie. It's still fun watching the set up and execution of the largely wafer thin characters as they are introduced to us only to be despatched mere minutes later.

Despite the heavy comedic presence in the script, however, once the third act kicks in the movie seems to decide that it wants to be a seriously scary trip after all, and we suddenly get a very effective sequence where Jason pursues one of the remaining counsellors. McLoughlin wheels out the old clichés of doors mysteriously creaking open on their own, the wind howling through the trees and long pregnant pauses. This doesn't detract from the fun, though, despite the fact that we know where this is all going, and the payoff when Jason finally strikes is still as sweet as ever.

Part VI : Jason Lives is another of my 'two beer' movies, best enjoyed by sinking a couple of beers while watching them and putting the brain into neutral. That isn't to insult it in any way, though. While I love cerebral movies like Se7en and (to a large extent) Candyman, sometimes you don't want steak and a good old burger and fries fits the bill magnificently (washed down with those couple of beers, naturally).

Jason Lives is pure hamburger, but extremely enjoyable for it. It's not the best in the series (that'd be the original), it doesn't have the highest body count (that honour goes to Jason X), but for my money it scores highest on that most important of the Saturday Night Fright Flick ratings, namely that it's a lot of fun.

## My Favourite Scene

The opening scene before the credits, as Tommy and his friend dig up Jason's coffin and then prise it open to reveal his maggot-infested corpse. Overcome by a fit of rage brought on by a flashback, Tommy grabs a metal fence pole and repeatedly impales Jason, leaving the pole sticking out of his corpse as he goes to get the gasoline he has brought along to burn the body.

However, as the wind blows and the clouds roll in, lightning strikes the pole and reanimates Jason. He crawls out of his grave and advances on Tommy who douses him with gasoline and goes to light a match. In a stroke of comedic genius the rain begins to fall just as he strikes it, at which point his friend swings a shovel at Jason that breaks over his head, doing no damage whatsoever.

Jason pushes Tommy's friend into the open grave, the coffin lid falling on top of him, and as Tommy flees to his truck, Jason picks up the hockey mask that Tommy had brought with him and puts it on. He picks up the metal fence pole and turns to look at the camera. He's back!

## Did You Know That...

For the scene in which Jason is hit by the paintballer, crew-member Dan Bradley was playing Jason, but when the studio saw his performance they asked for the role to be recast and C J Graham was brought in.

The shots of Jason being attacked with the boat propeller were shot in director Tom McLoughlin's parent's swimming pool.

# Halloween H20 (1998)

Directed by:   Steve Miner
Written by:   Robert Zappia
Starring:      Jamie Lee Curtis – Laurie Strode/Keri Tate
                Josh Hartnett – John Tate
                Michelle Williams – Molly Cartwell
                Adam Arkin – Will Brennan
                Jodi Lyn O'Keefe – Sarah Wainthrope
                LL Cool J – Ronald 'Ronnie' Jones
                Nancy Stephens – Marion Whittington
                Joseph Gordon-Levitt – Jimmy Holwell
                Janet Leigh – Norma Watson
                Chris Durand – Michael Myers

## Synopsis

Twenty years after the horrific events in Haddonfield, survivor Laurie Strode is living in California under an assumed name with her seventeen-year-old son John, having faked her death to escape from her murderous brother Michael Myers. However, Michael has other plans for Halloween this year, and sets about tracking her down, for one final showdown.

## Why I Love This Movie

Of all the many genre franchises Halloween has always been the one that I hold closest to my heart, and Michael Myers has always been top of my favourite maniacs list. Sure, I love Fred

Krueger, particularly in his first outing before he became a serial killing comedian, and Leatherface is very cool if a little limited in the personality stakes. Pinhead is hugely appealing, all S&M and damnation, but it is Michael Aubrey Myers (and with a middle name like that is it any wonder he turned out the way he did) who I hold most dear of our favourite movie monsters.

It may be a little surprising then that it isn't the original, and yes the best, Halloween that I have chosen for inclusion here. While I love John Carpenter's 1978 masterpiece with a passion bordering on obsession, I always find myself drawn to Halloween H20 because it manages to achieve more depth that any other horror movie I can think of has in recent years, with the exception perhaps of Wes Craven's innovative New Nightmare in 1994.

H20 blindsided me on its release. I had somehow managed to avoid reading anything about it and wasn't even aware of its existence until one night when I was on holiday in Florida with my girlfriend at the time and the trailer aired on the television. For two minutes I was enrapt. There could have been an atomic explosion three blocks away and I wouldn't have noticed as I watched with my jaw somewhere around my ankles as not only Michael Myers but also Laurie Strode paraded across the screen before me.

Needless to say I immediately declared that we would be going to the cinema that night, and pretty much ran to the hotel lobby to grab a copy of the local entertainments listings to find out where it was playing. A few hours later we found ourselves at a multiplex just off International Drive and for an hour and a half I was in heaven.

I digress, though. What I love about Halloween H20 is that it tackles the question of what happens in the long term to the survivors of our favourite maniacs. Once the villain is defeated and the credits roll that's usually the end of our relationship with Final Girl or Boy, unless they're back for the sequel of course, and even then it's rare that more than a year or two has passed since their last outing.

For Laurie Strode there has been no happy ever after following her night of terror twenty years previously. Even though logic suggests that her brother is dead, and that as her son John points out she herself saw him burn in the hospital at the end of Halloween II, she replies that she "didn't exactly stay to see his ashes" and so cannot shake the feeling that he is still out there (correctly, as it happens).

Just having Jamie Lee Curtis back in the series was a thrill for me (and many other Halloween fans) but the fact that she was back in a completely different light from the last time that we saw her, and that writer Robert Zappier obviously had huge respect for the series in creating a character with depth rather than just an updated rehash of the Laurie of the first movie had me in seventh heaven (or perhaps that should be seventh hell).

The scared, confused teenager of Halloween is no more, replaced by a paranoid, alcoholic woman who has been running from her demons for the last two decades, even going so far as to fake her death in a car crash and start a new life in California with her son. As far as she has run, though, there is no escape from Michael, who she sees in her dreams, in the reflections of shop windows, and even projecting his image onto others, as she does later in the movie when she thinks she sees him walking towards her when it is actually the school's guidance counsellor.

Zappier's intelligent script gives H20 a depth that previous entries in the series have sadly lacked (and let's not even talk about the comedy cops in Halloween 5, shall we?), and is also full of in jokes and references for the fans. In a scene that reflects the classroom scene in the original, Laurie (in the guise of Keri Tate, her new identity) is teaching about fate, using the example of Victor Frankenstein and his infamous creation, and about facing your monsters.

Molly, played by the talented Michelle Williams in her only genre outing to date, replies that Frankenstein finally faced his monster because he had nothing left to lose after his creation had killed off everybody that he loved, and that the confrontation was about redemption and fate. As a fan of the series it's this underlying theme that I really dig about the movie, the fact that Laurie is getting the opportunity after all these years to finally face down her nemesis and rid herself of the demons that have left her with a paranoia that threatens to engulf her son as well, the only thing she has left to lose.

It's not only Zappia's intelligent script that lifts this instalment above the others in the series, though. Director Steve Miner has clearly studied John Carpenter's original and infuses the movie with a sense of tension and dread, utilising long tracking shots and Carpenter's signature point of view camera work. He even has one scene at the beginning where Michael appears in the background of a shot as we focus on the character in the foreground – very effective stuff. This for me is the essence of what made Halloween such a groundbreaking movie back in 1978 and has kept it at the top of the favourite flicks lists over the years.

Whether prowling through the cramped confines of nurse Marion Whittington's home in the opening scenes, or through the expansive corridors and halls of Hillcrest Academy later on, Miner's camera keeps us on the edge of our seats throughout the relatively slow, but never plodding, first half and then cranks the dial up all the way in the third reel.

Great camera work and a decent script are nothing without a competent cast, though, and H20 was in the right place at the right time to be able to snag two leads who at the time were relatively unknown but have since gone onto great things. Josh Hartnett, in his first movie role and who has become one of the hottest young talents in the business, and Michelle Williams, who has since been nominated for a Best Supporting Actress Academy Award for her role in Brokeback Mountain, are completely believable as Laurie's son struggling to cope with his mother's paranoia, and his pretty and supportive girlfriend.

It's this gravitas that makes H20 one of my favourite horror movies, and gives the inevitable reappearance of Haddonfield's least favourite son a real sense of menace and terror as he stalks them, because unlike many of the teens that have appeared in genre slasher flicks I found myself actually giving a damn about what happened to them. This was true of the other characters as well, even LL Cool J's hapless security guard who provides the only real downside of the movie for me with Zappia's attempts at humour by way of having Cool J trying to write a romantic novel and relaying his efforts over the phone to his girl.

For me the worlds of rap and Halloween should never mix, but what makes Cool J bearable here, as opposed to just plain annoying like Buster Rhymes in Halloween : Resurrection, is that he has a genuine screen presence and, as he proved in 1999's Deep Blue Sea, can actually act.

This is a minor quibble, though, which doesn't taint the rest of the movie, and is more than made up for in the clever references to previous mythology and to other genre flicks that Zappia has peppered his script with.

I love when sequels tie in closely to what has gone before, and so despite the fact that Halloweens 3 through 6 are ignored, apart from a brief reference to Laurie's supposed death in a car crash that also formed the basis of the explanation as to why Jamie Lee wasn't in Halloween 4, I found myself loving what Zappia had brought to the party.

With the obvious unavailability of the late Donald Pleasance, Zappia pulled a masterstroke in effectively bringing closure to the Loomis arc by having Michael pay Marion Whittington, his nurse from the original movie, a visit to find out where Laurie is hiding. After her demise, the titles run over footage of Loomis's old office, the walls covered in maps, drawings and photographs that very effectively convey the extent of his obsession with Michael.

In a nod to the original concept of Halloween there is a newspaper article with the headline 'Babysitter Killer On The Loose', and on top of the mess of papers there lies a framed black and white photograph of the late Sam Loomis. There's also a very effective voiceover recreating Loomis's greatest speeches about Michael Myers that tells us all we need to know about him (although sadly it's not Donald Pleasance's voice, but rather that of veteran voiceover artist Tom Kane.)

I also love that the police are well aware of the old babysitter murders, so much so that they have become the stuff of urban legend. This is particularly highlighted when Laurie is trying to tell her partner of her real, hidden life, and he initially thinks she is having him on and playing along with the old Michael Myers myth.

The best thing about H20, though, is that in bucking the trend of most other sequels where our favourite maniacs become less potent and even parodies of themselves (I'm looking at you Fred), Michael Myers is just as cold and chilling as he ever was. Thanks to a combination of Zappia not putting him in any ridiculous situations, and a solid physical performance from stuntman Chris Durand, every time Michael is on screen you can't help but be transfixed by him.

The intelligence that is part of Michael's character comes across perfectly as well. He is no brainless killer, but rather a canny force of nature who is completely focused on his quest. There is a scene at a remote rest stop where he has to steal a car, but rather than just wade in and butcher the driver and her daughter, he knows exactly what he needs, the keys to her car, and takes only those. As he leaves the restroom there is a chillingly effective shot where as the woman watches Michael through a crack in the door he stops, turning his head towards her to look directly into her eyes, before moving on. He has no need to kill her, so he just continues on his unrelenting mission.

Halloween H20 is a perfect Saturday Night Fright Flick. It's intelligent, scary and a Halloween fan's dream as it reunites Laurie Strode and her brother in a believable way after all those years. It's not the classic that the original is, but still very much a worthy continuation of the series and my favourite sequel, though Halloween II comes in a close second.

## My Favourite Scene

I have two here, but they share a common theme; the interaction between Laurie and Michael.

The first is a brief moment after Michael has been trying to kill John and Molly, having trapped them in a porch. After hammering on the door Laurie lets them in just as Michael opens the outer gate and slams the door behind them. She then looks through the round porthole window and finds herself face to face with her brother for the first time in twenty years. The few moments that the camera holds on this are magical as Michael performs his signature tilt of the head and Laurie stares at him with frightened yet defiant eyes.

The second is the final moments of the confrontation between Laurie and Michael at the end of the movie. Again they find themselves face to face, and he holds out his hand to her. She stretches hers towards his, as if feeling the family connection for a moment, but then withdraws and finally lays her demons to rest.

(However, and I won't give anything away here for those who haven't seen it, this final scene is something of a misdirection given the revelations at the beginning of Resurrection, but even knowing that on repeat viewings, I still remember the first time I saw this scene on H20's release, and because of that this scene still retains its' initial power for me.)

## Did You Know That...

Laurie's secretary in the movie, Norma, is played by Janet Leigh, Jamie Leigh's real life mother, and star of Hitchcock's 1963 classic Psycho. Her name is a nod to Anthony Perkins's 'mother' persona.

There are two other Psycho connections. The car Norma stands in front of while talking to Laurie is the same model that she drove and was ultimately buried in, and the music playing in the background in this scene is also a riff on the Psycho sound-track.

When Laurie tells John to "go down the street to the Becker's", this not only references her "go down the street to the McKenzie's" line in the original, but also Drew Barrymore's homage to this line in Scream. Barrymore's character was called Casey Becker.

Scream writer Kevin Williamson wrote a treatment for the movie which was ultimately not used, but is rumoured to be the basis for the final filmed version.

A clip from Scream 2 is playing on the television in one scene, and is a nod to the use of clips from Halloween in the original Scream.

Executive Producer Moustapha Akkad originally intended for the Michael Myers to be a copycat killer in H20, and that the reason for this would be explained in the following Halloween movie. This idea was ultimately dropped though in favour of a completely different explanation for Michael's reappearance in 2002's Halloween : Resurrection (and if you want to know what it is, go rent the movie! On second thoughts, don't - it's rubbish.)

# I Know What You Did Last Summer (1997)

Directed by:   Jim Gillespie
Written by:   Kevin Williamson
Starring:   Jennifer Love Hewitt – Julie James
   Sarah Michelle Geller – Helen
   Freddy Prinze Jr – Ray
   Ryan Phillipe - Barry

## Synopsis

After running over a man on a deserted highway, four teen-agers with their futures at stake if they report it decide to dispose of the body and pretend it never happened.

One year later, they receive a letter from someone claiming to know what they did last summer. As they desperately try to figure out who knows their secret the bodies begin to pile up.

## Why I Love This Movie

I have a confession to make. I used to watch Dawson's Creek.

There, it's out in the open but what does this have to do with a book on horror movies and a teen slasher flick starring Buffy The Vampire Slayer, I hear you ask. Well, one of things that I liked so much about Dawson's Creek was that the dialogue that came out of the teenagers mouths actually sounded realistic, and the main reason for this was because it was came from the pen of one Kevin Williamson.

Though Dawson's Creek didn't debut until 1998, the reason it was a draw for me was thanks to Williamson having written both 1996's Scream, which is discussed elsewhere in this book, and I Know What You Did Last Summer. IKWYDLS works for me on many levels, and while it gets knocked a lot in horror circles, largely I'm sure because of the appalling mess that passes for a sequel, I think the harsh criticism is a little unfair, and that this is actually one of the best teen slasher movies of the 1990s.

One major plus point as far as I'm concerned is the setting. For some reason I just love movies that are set in small American coastal resorts. Maybe it's because I've always lived in big cities, or maybe it all harks back to Jaws, which had a big effect on me at an early age, but if you set your movie on the coast then I'll be lining up for a ticket, no questions asked. This is why I've seen The Lost Boys so many times, apart from the fact that it's a great movie of course, and why I was entranced by the short lived Point Pleasant series.

IKWYDLS is so much more than just a pretty location, though. Playing with one of my other great movie loves, the urban legend, Williamson takes the classic maniac with a hook myth and breathes new life into it by continuing the trend that he virtually invented in Scream of making the characters aware of horror movie clichés, and then coming up with brand new clichés in order to kill them off.

For example, the scene that introduces us to our four leads has them sitting on a beach at night literally telling campfire stories. As we join them they're discussing which of the variations on the maniac with a hook story is actually the real one, even going so far as to have one of the characters point out that the story isn't actually real and is in fact nothing more than an urban legend. This scene, incidentally, reminds me of a similar opening scene on a beach in Gary Sherman's underrated 1981 classic Dead And Buried.

Williamson also gives his characters enough intelligence to realise the consequences of their actions, and so makes the scene where they are discussing their options after having mown down a man on a coastal road after their alcohol and drug fuelled beach party all the more convincing. There are credible pros and cons as to whether they should report it, but with too much to lose collectively, having just graduated high school and about to head out into the world to begin their adult lives, they decide to cover it up and move on, swearing to take their secret to the grave, which let's face it is just inviting trouble to come a-knocking.

One thing that's always intrigued me about slasher movies is that after the prologue, the action almost invariable jumps forward to 'One Year Later', or 'Ten Years Later' or some such precise measure of time. Is there some handbook for psychopaths that states you must wait a year, or ten years, before you're allowed to take your revenge on the world? What's wrong with 'A Couple of Weeks Later', or 'Some Time Later'? Halloween 5 was the best example of this, asking us to believe that Michael Myers had lay motionless in that run down shack for exactly one year before resuming his killing spree. Ridiculous, but of course we bought it unquestioningly.

One year later it is, though, and despite the fact that we have no idea what the Fisherman has been up to for that year, Williamson actually gives him a credible reason to be stalking our teen quartet. He also adds another perspective to their crime by having the girls visit the sister of their victim to try and discover who might be out to kill them, and in doing so he reveals the devastating effect that their actions have had on his family.

Eschewing the traditional cliché of having the stalked characters pull together when faced with being filleted by a maniac fisherman, the year gap has seen the two young couples both break up acrimoniously, and all four of them go off in different directions. Helen's dream of modelling in New York has crashed and burned leaving her ineptly running the perfume department in the family department store, while Ray has succumbed to his father's legacy and become a fisherman. (Hang on, isn't the killer a fisherman? Nah, that'd be too easy, wouldn't it?) As a result the dynamic between the four leads is initially strained, and feels every bit as realistic as a forced reunion after a bad break-up would in reality.

What makes this movie a winner for me is that despite being a riff on the old slasher movie conventions – set up the premise, spend an hour misdirecting the audience as to who may be the killer, and then for the last twenty minutes rack up the body count before the final reveal – director Jim Gillespie does it with such style that it grabs your attention and doesn't let go until the credits roll.

Yes, there are a couple of scenes where logic takes a comfort break, but I never said this was a perfect movie. For example, while stalking a victim through the department store, somewhat appropriately called Shiver's, why on earth, aside from the fact that it looks great on camera and delivers a solid scare, would the killer drape himself in polythene and pretend to be a mannequin? And how, after dumping a body in the trunk of Julie's car along with several dozen crabs, does the killer managed to remove it, and the crabs, in the minute or so that it takes Julie to bring the rest of the gang running to see it? Not to mention the fact that below the decks of the killer's boat, the engine room and storage area, complete with tons of ice and the obligatory body or two, seem to be considerably larger than the available space.

However, as fans of the genre we regular forgive these illogical plot devices because we're there for one thing, the kills. In that department IKWYDLS delivers. Though he hasn't got the imaginative and extensive repertoire of Freddy or Jason, one thing the Fisherman does have is sheer brutality. The first on screen kill sees him slamming his hook up through the chin of his victim and dragging him forcefully across a table. Actually, slamming his hook into various parts of various bodies is pretty much his trademark, but one that works well.

I Know What You Did Last Summer delivers on virtually all of the levels that a horror movie should. The characters are believable, as is the plot (well, mostly), and it moves along at a decent pace until the last twenty minutes when it goes ever so slightly off the boil but not enough to stop it being an entertaining Saturday Night Fright Flick.

The bottom line on this movie, though, is that it's good fun, and intelligent fun at that. IKWYDLS is the movie that made Jennifer Love Hewitt a scream queen for ten minutes and proved that Sarah Michelle Geller had more than just Buffy in her repertoire. It is a fine example of the post-modern ironic teen slasher (or whatever you want to call this particular genre) and one you should do yourself a favour and see if you haven't already. Just make sure you avoid the lame sequels.

**My Favourite Scene**

After being chased though her family's department store by the Fisherman, Helen throws herself out of a second floor window and lands in a narrow tyre lined alley. A hundred yards away she can see the annual parade that she has just been a part of passing by and heads towards safety.

Twenty feet from the main road and the marching band that is filing past, she stops to check behind her. The Fisherman suddenly jumps her and sets to work with his hook as the camera switches to an overhead shot that shows him carrying out his work on the right hand side of the screen while the marching band files past on the left hand side.

The irony of her being so close to safety and then being hacked to pieces just yards from salvation makes for a great shot and an imaginative kill.

**Did You Know That...**

The film originally had a different ending, but this was re-shot for the final cut. It wasn't wasted, however, as it was used for the teaser trailer.

The original trailer claimed that the movie was 'from the creator of Scream'. Miramax, the owners of the Scream franchise successfully sued Miramax for false advertising and the phrase was removed.

In the movie the group goes down to 'Dawson's Beach', a nod to the hit television teen drama Dawson's Creek which Kevin Williamson was writing at the time.

Jennifer Love Hewitt is also a successful singer as well as an actress, and has released several critically acclaimed albums.

The movie spawned two sequels, neither of which are likely to make any future volumes of Saturday Night Fright Flicks.

# Jeepers Creepers (2001)

Directed by:  Victor Salva
Written by:  Victor Salva
Starring:     Gina Philips – Trish Jenner
              Justin Long – Darry Jenner
              Jonathon Breck – The Creeper
              Patricia Belcher – Jezelle Gay Hartman
              Eileen Brennan – The Cat Lady

## Synopsis

After being vehicularly harrassed in the middle of nowhere by a maniac in a beaten up old truck, siblings Trish and Darry later see the driver dumping what appear to be bodies down a pipe. He spots them and gives chase, running them off the road before speeding off into the distance.

When they return to see whether there are any survivors they discover that the reality of their situation is far worse than they could have imagined, and with the help of an eccentric psychic learn that they are now the main targets for a seemingly unstoppable monster.

## Why I Love This Movie

As with many of the movies in this book, Jeepers Creepers isn't likely to make the top ten of the greatest horror movies ever made, but Victor Salva's commercial breakthrough is undeniably one of those great, cheesy, two-beer flicks that are perfect Saturday Night Fright Flick fodder.

I was already very familiar with Salva for two reasons, one good, one the polar opposite. The good reason was that I loved two of his previous movies, 1989's underground classic Clownhouse, a creepy tale of psychotic clowns that will put you off the circus for life, and 1995's highly underrated Powder, a powerful and moving tale of an albino boy which I have to admit brings a tear to my eye whenever I watch it. The bad reason was his conviction on child abuse charges for soliciting oral sex from a minor during the filming of Clownhouse. Thanks to that I will never have a shred of respect for Salva the man, but Salva the director definitely knows what he's doing behind the camera, as is very apparent from Jeepers Creepers.

While I'm very much a purist when it comes to actually owning movies on DVD, and Jeepers Creepers is no exception, this was actually the first of a very few number of movies that I have ever downloaded, thanks mainly to the buzz it was stirring up in Fangoria. At the time, horror movies weren't always guaranteed a theatrical release here in England, the current renaissance not really kicking in until the success of the Texas Chain-Saw Massacre remake in 2003, so being keen to see what all the fuss was about I downloaded it and was suitably impressed, so much so that I saw it again at the cinema when it was released and then picked it up the first day it was released on DVD.

One thing that sets Jeepers Creepers apart from a lot of the usual horror movie fare for me is the fact that the two main characters are actually likeable. Darry and Trisha, played by Justin Long and Gina Philips, are very believable as the homeward bound siblings who tease and bitch about each other, but have an endearing underlying solidarity that allows us to genuinely care about what happens to them.

Salva adeptly captures the little nuances that occur between siblings, whether down to their game of making amusing phrases out of license plates or insulting each other without repeating themselves, and really breathes life into the characters.

Another major plus point for this movie is Salva's ability to create tension and atmosphere. After gently easing us into the movie for the first ten minutes, during which time the only other characters we meet are an old couple driving an RV, he plays a masterstroke by having the camera sit on the bonnet as Darry and Trisha drive and chat, while in the background the RV turns off to reveal another truck way back in the distance.

As they continue to talk this truck grows closer and closer, the siblings oblivious to what is happening in their rear view mirror, until suddenly the truck accelerates and is right on their bumper, honking its horn like an enraged hornet.

At this point, the movie effectively becomes Spielberg's Duel for ten minutes or so as the Creeper rides their bumper and tries to run them off the road. There's a fine line between homage and rip off, but Salva manages to stay on the right side of the road, and even got Richard Matheson, who wrote the original story that Spielberg based Duel on, to appear in a short clip in an easter egg on the Jeepers Creepers DVD.

Salva uses the same technique later in the movie when a police car is following Darry and Trisha and, as they chat in the foreground, through the rear window we see the Creeper land atop the cop car and take out the two police officers inside, literally pulling them out of the car.

The end of this particular sequence gives rise to a great visual gag as the Creeper does something deliciously disgusting (watch the movie and see!) to the severed head of one of the cops, while flanked in the background by a billboard advertising a brand of meat with the slogan 'Tastes So Darn Good'

As for atmosphere, Salva makes full use of the movie's woodland location. Many of the scenes in the first third of the movie are set against beautiful shots of the trees lining the road, giving the impression that Darry and Trisha are out in the back of beyond and well beyond any kind of conventional police help. This is another of the things that I personally really dig about this movie, due to the fact that I'm a big fan of backwoods horror movies like Wrong Turn, The Hills Have Eyes and of course the grandpappy of them all, Tobe Hooper's 1974 classic Texas Chain-Saw Massacre.

As well as the natural surroundings, Salva makes the most of the superb sets in the movie. An old boarded up church that Darry and Trisha first come across when investigating the pipe they had seen the Creeper dumping his bodies down is supremely creepy. Thanks to a large contingent of noisy crows perched on the roof, and subtle details like the damaged cross atop the steeple, this is one of those classic horror movie locations that feel menacing without having to really do anything.

However, there is more to the church than just birds and broken crosses. After Darry finds himself at the wrong end of a long pipe, he discovers my favourite set of the movie, the Creeper's lair. This set blew my mind when I first saw it. Imagine Leatherface being commissioned to create a copy of the Sistine Chapel. The walls and ceiling are covered with petrified, stitched together bodies. A blood stained table is surrounded with the usual furnishings of these crazy psycho killer types – bottles of coloured liquids, various sharp, rusty implements, cobwebs and, oh yes, blood. Lots of it.

Sure, this is all a cliché, and to be honest there's not much about Jeepers Creepers that *is* particularly original, but sometimes you just want to pull on that old familiar sweater and settle into something that feels like home. The other two major locations fit this description to a tee. The cat lady's house is your typical isolated, run down, single storey farmhouse in the middle of nowhere. Creepy scarecrow? Check. Eccentric old lady? Check. Lots of cats? Well, OK, not that conventional in horror movies, but certainly consistent with the eccentric old lady character.

Likewise the police station. Salva pulls off one very creepy scene when Trisha, trying to hold it together, has her face pressed up against a mirror in one of the rooms. However, the mirror is a one-way mirror, and we see the Creeper with his face pressed up against the transaparent side, just inches from Trisha, watching her intently while she is blissfully unaware of the situation.

By this point, we know exactly what the Creeper is and why he does what he does. Now I have to be honest and confess that I was one of the people who upon initially watching the movie thought that the first half was fantastic but the second half, once the 'secret' of the Creeper was revealed was a bit lame. However, having seen this movie several times now, I actually like what it does and the how it unfolds. Sure, I still think that building on the extremely effective and tense first half, Salva should have kept the Creeper firmly rooted in reality, but then we'd have been revisiting the old 'backwoods' territory which has been done in other genre classics. So, by doing what he did with the script, Salva actually brought something new (well, new-ish) to the party.

I even like the psychic woman, Jezelle Gay Hartman, played by Patricia Belcher, who I thought was a completely unnecessary plot device on first seeing the movie and should have been left on the cutting room floor. However, on repeated viewings the whole psychic element adds to the fun, as she comes into the picture with information that one of the leads isn't going to make it, but crucially doesn't tell us who. This efectively cranks up the tension as we wonder which of the Jenner kids will buy the farm (although oddly enough, the one who does actually returns in the sequel while the one who doesn't, doesn't).

Not to give anything away for those of you who haven't seen the movie yet, the ending is wonderfully bleak, and features one of those final shots that, while not a jumper like the one in Carrie, will definitely stay with you for a while.

Oh, one last thing. If you enjoyed this movie, and if it's not too late, avoid the sequel. It's OK, but you're better off watching this one again.

**My Favourite Scene**

After landing on the top of a police car that is following Darry and Trisha's car, the Creeper pulls one cop out of the side window and peels the roof open like a sardine tin to decapitate the other. Having done so, he tosses the head onto the bonnet of the Jenner's car and both vehicles skid to a halt.

As they watch, transfixed, the Creeper climbs out of the police car, picks up the head and proceeds to pull the tongue out of it using his teeth. What makes the scene really work, though, is that this happens against the backdrop of a giant billboard advertising meat with the slogan 'Tastes So Darn Good'. Classic horror movie black humour.

**Did You Know That...**

Gina Phillips appeared in 13 episodes of season three of Ally McBeal, playing a character called Sandy Hingle.

Victor Salva originally wrote the role of the Creeper for Lance Henriksen, who had appeared in his 1995 movie Powder.

Eileen Brennan, who played the Cat Lady, was a regular on Rowan & Martin's Laugh In back in 1968.

Justin Long assured his place in celluloid history by appearing alongside Bruce Willis in the fourth Die Hard movie, 2007's Live Free Or Die Hard (aka Die Hard 4.0).

# The Omen (1976)

Directed by:   Richard Donner
Written by:    David Seltzer
Starring:       Gregory Peck – Robert Thorn
                Lee Remick – Katherine Thorn
                David Warner – Keith Jennings
                Billie Whitelaw – Mrs Baylock
                Harvey Stephens – Damien Thorn

## Synopsis

After his son is stillborn in a Rome hospital, high flying American politician Robert Thorn agrees to covertly adopt another boy whose mother died in childbirth, raising the boy as his own. Upon moving to England, however, a series of strange events and horrific deaths lead him to team up with a obsessed photographer who slowly persuades him that his son may not be all that he seems.

## Why I Love This Movie

This is another movie, like Carrie before it, that I had persuaded my parents to let me stay up and watch on television. If I remember correctly it was 1980 or thereabouts and my appetite for all things horror was growing at a healthy, or should that be unhealthy, rate. I was devouring any horror novels that I could get my hands on, usually courtesy of my friend Nick's dad, who had lent me the hardback of Stephen King's The Shining when I was nine, and about which my primary school teacher at the time had remarked "This is a little strong, isn't it," after spying it in my school bag and flicking through it.

I don't actually remember much about that initial viewing, but the many times that I've subsequently seen it over the years have ensured that my deep and lasting love affair with this movie still burns brightly to this day. This is one of those movies that given the premise - a high flying American politician unwittingly raises the Anti-Christ - should never have been either as entertaining or as successful as it was. Somehow, though, it pulls it off, and then some.

For me the key to this success can be split four ways. First up for a big pat on the back is writer David Seltzer for creating a script that is both intelligent and entertaining, a rare combination. Seltzer did a ton of research about the Anti-Christ, Armageddon and all things religious for this movie, and it shows in the script. In less capable hands this movie could have become a mess of exposition and metaphor, witness any of the cheap knock-offs and pale imitations that followed its success, but in Seltzer's hands this is all lovingly crafted into a story that roots this unlikely and improbable premise firmly in reality, and makes it plausible. I bought every minute of it.

The second round of props go to director Richard Donner. There's not an ounce of fat on this movie. Every second of screen time is used to maximum effect. Case in point being the first ten minutes. In this short screen time Donner takes us from the opening credits through the switching of the infants in the Rome hospital, the establishing of the Thorns as a happy family unit, the news that Thorn is being transferred to London as the new Ambassador to Great Britain, and finally to the opening shots of Damien's fifth birthday party. Yet, none of this feels rushed.

The third round of applause is for composer Jerry Goldsmith's often imitated score. Without his inventive and extremely effective use of chanting and operatic instrumentation it is debatable whether the movie would have had the same impact. Music in movies is a factor often overlooked, but here Goldsmith nails it to the wall.

The opening credits, which feature a static silhouette of Damien, his shadow forming the iconic upside down cross motif, and a series of names that flash up in quick succession instils an air of foreboding and menace every time I watch them. As the soundtrack builds its layers of chanting and ultimately segues into the opening shots of Rome's rain lashed streets as Thorn prepares to make the worst decision of his life, it conjures up images of Dario Argento's work. High praise indeed.

The fourth and final tip of my hat goes to the cast, and what a stellar collection of names Donner managed to assemble for his movie. Thanks to the allure of Seltzer's intelligent script we get to see some of the finest acting talent known to man do themselves proud. Acting legend and respected veteran Gregory Peck brings a believable gravitas to the role of Robert Thorn. In lesser hands the slow realisation that his son is in fact the Anti-Christ may not have rung true or been convincing, but I completely bought Peck's performance.

A lot of this is down to the subtle looks he gives David Warner's character Jennings as he attempts to convince him that Armageddon is just around the corner. One instance of this occurs while the two men are driving towards the scene of one of the movie's most effective set pieces and Warner is reading from the book of Revelations. As he does so, Peck turns to look at him, a simple yet slight movement of the head, but it speaks volumes, those volumes saying "Are you insane?"

David Warner is extremely watchable in pretty much anything he appears in, but his portrayal of the photographer Jennings is surely one of the brightest jewels in his thespian crown. Utterly convincing as an everyman, in subsequent scenes in his darkroom he first smokes then swigs from a beer can, he manages to make the expositional dialogue about the Anti-Christ, Armageddon and dodgy prophetic photographs (a plot device that has turned up numerous times in subsequent years, most notably in Final Destination 3). This man could make even the most implausible conspiracy sound rational.

Lee Remick is great as Thorn's self-centred wife Katherine. After being unceremoniously knocked over a first floor balcony by young Damien, Peck asks her "Do you think we should call a doctor?" to which she replies "No, it's just a couple of bruises." Peck shoots her another of his marvellously withering looks, telling her, "I meant for Damien."

Later in the movie she is lying in bed and Peck asks her if she thinks there is anything wrong with Damien. "What could be wrong with him," she replies, a puzzled look on her face, "We're beautiful people aren't we?" Priceless. This after an early scene in the movie where she strolls arm in arm with her husband alongside a fast moving stream and seems not to notice or care that their two year old devil child has fallen some way behind them.

Then there's Billie Whitelaw who plays surely the most evil nanny ever committed to celluloid. Move over Rebecca De Mornay, you've got nothing on Mrs Baylock. She doesn't so much rock the cradle as warp the timber with her milk-curdling looks, the best of which comes just before Mrs Thorn takes a final swan dive into an ambulance, spectacularly blowing out the windows and doors as she lands.

Of course, a movie about the Anti-Christ needs its very own little bastard child, and Harvey Stevens delivers in spades. From the first moment I saw him on screen he had me utterly convinced that he was trouble with a capital T. Donner knew he was on to a good thing, too, when Stevens hit him in the cajones during his audition! Kids in movies usually come across as being extremely wooden (which is fine if you're playing Pinocchio, but witness Mannequin Skywalker in The Phantom Menace), but Harvey Stevens was born to play this role (did anyone think to check under *his* hairline?).

For me, though, the real appeal of the movie can be distilled down to three key scenes. The first is David Warner's now classic demise. Richard Donner proved that he could be a bastard to the audience with weaker stomachs here by noting that most people hid their eyes for two seconds during on screen deaths, and then lingering on Warner's spinning cranium for twice as long. A textbook example of how to execute a set piece kill . Many have tried to get it *this* right, but very few have succeeded.

The second is after Patrick Troughton's repentant priest Father Brennan has confronted Robert Thorn. As he walks away Donner masterfully begins to slowly build a maelstrom of wind and leaves that buffet the priest. The tension is turned up to eleven as Troughton forces his way through the gale, his cross held aloft as lightning strikes a tree, severing a bough, and he bangs on the locked doors of a church. After a couple of intense minutes, Donner despatches Troughton with another bolt of lighting that ironically sends the church's lightning rod slamming through him, pinning him to the ground.

The third scene, rounding out my unholy trinity of kick ass scenes, is possibly one of my favourite sequences ever in horror movies. This scene, where Peck and Warner travel to the graveyard where Damien's mother is supposedly buried, positively drips with atmosphere as Donner all but kills the sound for several minutes, letting the visuals do the talking. From the moment we see the graveyard it's obvious that this is one bad place. Drawing the scene out at a deliciously slow pace, Donner lets us into the shocking revelation of what is actually in the two graves and then suddenly introduces a low growl to the soundtrack, switching to the point of view of a huge Doberman.

As if the tension with the dogs and the truth about Damien's mother and Thorn's real son isn't enough, Donner ensures that having brought us to the edge of our seats he gives us a swift kick to the floor by having Peck impale his arm on the spiked railings of the cemetery as they try and escape. Despite not being particularly graphic or gory, this makes me wince every time. Thanks, Richard.

I could go on and on about the cool sequences in The Omen – the nanny's suicide, the uncomfortable endgame in a church with Thorn and the daggers, the visit to another church early on in the picture, the berserk monkeys in the safari park - but the one I must mention before I wrap The Omen up is the final scene.

The original ending had all three Thorns being buried, but in an inspired change of heart, Donner instead slowly zooms in on Damien standing between the President and the First Lady, holding their hands as his adopted parents are given a military funeral. That final shot of Harvey Stephens turning to look at the camera, and then breaking into *that* grin was the icing on the cake for this picture. You can keep all your last minute shock revelations and twist endings (though the bloody hand in Carrie can stay), because that one little smile chilled the marrow in my bones and is the perfect ending to this awesome Saturday Night Fright Flick.

## My Favourite Scene

As mentioned above, definitely the scene in the graveyard at Cerveteri. As Thorn and Jennings approach the locked gates, the soundtrack silent but for the crunching of their shoes on the gravel, the rustling of the wind through the trees and the chirping of nocturnal insects, we feel a growing sense of unease. The cemetery itself is beautifully backlit by the moon shining through the clouds and Donner makes very effective use of some imaginative shots to give us the impression that they might not be alone.

Suddenly Jennings calls out as he finds the grave they're looking for and it is now that Thorn finally begins to accept that all is not well, and that Jennings and Father Brennan might not be as crazy as he thought.

Then we hear the panting and we just know something bad is about to go down here. Jerry Goldsmith's score begins to build as the men lift the lid of the tomb and discover the skeleton of Damien's real mother, and then the true fate of his son. As the truth sinks in, the men look up as we hear a deep growling and discover that several huge Dobermans are surrounding them.

A chase for the exit ensues, with both men being dragged to the ground along the way amid a flurry of limbs and teeth, the soundtrack exploding with barks and growls as they eventually make their way over the spiked railings, but not unscathed. This is a tremendous scene that is not only atmospheric but genuinely scary and unsettling.

**Did You Know That...**

More than twice the movie's original $2.8 million budget was spent on promoting and advertising it. It went on to gross over $60 million in the United States alone.

Director Richard Donner went on to make Superman The Movie (1978), The Goonies (1985) and all four Lethal Weapon movies. He also shot a good portion of uncredited footage for Superman II (1980) but was sacked and replaced by Richard Lester. Donner's director's cut has subsequently been released on DVD and makes for an interesting look at how two different directors view the same movie. Another example of this is the two very different versions of the recent Exorcist prequels.

Charlton Heston, Roy Schneider and William Holden all turned down the role of Robert Thorn before it was offered to Gregory Peck. William Holden did accept the role of Richard Thorn, however, in the 1978 sequel Damien : Omen II.

Harvey Stephens made only one more movie after The Omen, 1980's Guaguin The Savage, and then retired from the movie business.

# Opera (1987)

Directed by:  Dario Argento
Written by:  Dario Argento
Starring:  Christina Marsillach – Betty
Ian Charleson – Marco
Urbano Barberini – Inspector Alan Santini
Daria Nicolodi – Mira

## Synopsis

After the lead in a new production of Verdi's Macbeth is involved in an accident, the young understudy is given her chance to step into the starring role.

It soon becomes apparent, though, that she has a crazed fan, who forces her to watch the murders of her friends, and that the key to uncovering the maniac's identity may lay in her recurring nightmares from her youth.

## Why I Love This Movie

You can't write a book about horror flicks without including at least one movie by Italian giallo maestro Dario Argento. Though a much loved director within the genre, Argento's movies are often criticised as being style over substance, with plot logic taking a backseat to the visuals and undeniably stunning cinematography that permeates much of his work.

Although a big fan of his work I do have to agree up to a point, and Opera does fall foul of this criticism, but sometimes a horror movie needs to be stylish, and to be filmed with enthusiasm, flair and flamboyancy. (See also Argento's Suspiria as a great example of this maxim.)

On this count Opera succeeds magnificently, Argento proudly wearing his style on his bloody sleeve from the very first shot of the opera house, reflected in an extreme close up of a raven's pitch black eye. The opening few minutes, set to a rousing opera score are superbly executed, with the protestations of the show's diva ringing out over the music and the cawing of the ravens.

We never see the diva herself, 'The Great' Mara Czekova, as she first assaults one of the ravens before flouncing out of the opera house followed by her fawning assistant and entourage, who we see from her point of view, before emerging into the street and being involved in an accident.

It's these POV shots that lie at the heart of Opera's appeal, Argento putting us in the shoes of the killer as he prowls the corridors and backstage areas of the opera house before emerging in a box high above the auditorium to watch the object of his obsession, the understudy Betty who has been thrust into the starring role thanks to Mara Czekova's accident. (Or was it? C'mon, this is Argento we're talking about here.)

Not content to merely make us voyeurs, though, Argento retains the POV shots for the most memorable murder of the movie, and possibly of his career, and actually casts us in the role of killer. Though perhaps not his best movie - that accolade in my humble opinion still goes to Deep Red (aka Profundo Rosso) even after all these years - Opera is certainly in the running for being his most brutal.

In my favourite death scene from Argento's oeuvre, the killer ties our heroine to a pillar and tapes a number of needles under her eyes, telling her that 'if you try to close your eyes you'll tear them apart, so you'll just have to watch everything'. As she tries not to blink, causing drops of blood to bead on the needles, we are placed in the killer's POV as her companion returns from fetching drinks, and become accomplices to murder as he drives a huge knife up into the victim's mouth. Following an extreme close up of the tip of the blade actually moving about inside the mouth, we effectively become the killer as the victim raises his hands to the screen to fend off the rain of knife blows, all seen from our point of view.

The sequence is over in a matter of seconds, but the fact Argento makes us complicit in the killing, intercutting with close ups of Betty's eyeball and the close proximity of the needles to it, and a couple of extremely effective shots from her POV looking through the needles at her companion, makes this uncomfortable sequence seem to go on for much longer than it actually does.

This is no scene for the faint-hearted, particularly those with an aversion to anything involving eyes and sharp objects, and always reminds me of the infamous splinter scene in fellow Italian Lucio Fulci's 1979 classic Zombie Flesh Eaters, more of which elsewhere in this book. Though there have undoubtedly been more brutal and graphic onscreen murders, thanks to Argento's twisted mind virtually putting the knife in my hand this one has remained with me over the years.

This is by no means an isolated moment of bloody terror in the movie, though. Argento really went to town on this flick and delivers a number of gruesome set pieces (depending of course on whether you see an unrated version of the movie or not), including a graphic head/coat hook interface that is reminiscent of a similar death in Fulci's The Beyond (aka Seven Doors of Death), an eye gouging, a couple of stabbings, an imaginative use of scissors for a vicious tracheotomy, and one of the most stylish shootings I've ever seen in a movie (and which is my favourite scene in the movie, so more on this shortly).

Visuals aside, Argento plays the movie's trump card with his superb use of sound. While other movies may be content to use light and shadow, and of course gore, to unnerve the viewer, Argento manages to get under our skin by accentuating the screeching of a blade as it drags across the surface of a mirror, or the rattling of scissor blades against teeth as the killer tries to retrieve something (*what* would be telling if you haven't seen it) from his victim's mouth, before the coup de grace of the afore-mentioned tracheotomy. Here the killer takes a huge pair of dressmaking scissors and with great deliberation cuts through the flesh of his victim's neck.

We see none of the gory detail onscreen, though. Instead Argento shows us the killer's gloved hand working the scissors, accompanied by a deliciously wet, crunching sound, allowing our imagination to fill in the visual blanks.

It's an extremely effective technique, reminiscent of Tobe Hooper's original 1973 Texas Chain-Saw Massacre, which people always seem to recall as being far more bloody and violent than it actually is. A perfect example of less being more in the mind of the audience.

As befits a movie set in an opera house, Argento's extensive use of opera music adds greatly to the atmosphere. There are several long sections in the movie where the only sound is that of the opera itself, leaving the visuals to tell the story, the movie almost becoming an opera itself.

This works particularly well as the ravens come into their own towards the climax of the movie, Argento giving us a literal birds eye view of the opera house as the camera dives and swoops around the beautiful building. We start up high, and in a series of technically stunning shots, dive down towards the audience, passing inches above their heads in an inspired sequence that I have yet to see replicated, let alone bettered.

The most effective use of sound is the harsh cawing of the ravens. In a series of well-edited shots Argento manages to very effectively turn them into credible supporting characters, which gives their pivotal role in the movie's climax an air of believability. In fact, the ravens actually exude more charisma on the screen than one or two of their human co-stars.

Ironically, just as the characters in Argento's movie seem to fall prey to the curse of Macbeth, so does the logic of the movie's script. The first ninety minutes of Opera are eminently watchable and contain all the elements of a perfect Saturday

Night Fright Flick, but for reasons known only to Argento these last ten minutes suddenly veer off into left field following the revelation of the killer's identity and motivation.

Having managed to maintain just enough substance to justify the admittedly impressive style for the majority of the picture, the last ten minutes stretch first credibility and then believability as our heroine spends the dying moments of the movie behaving completely out of character. Thankfully this doesn't ruin the Opera experience and is a minor complaint, along with the occasional outbreak of Dutch Elm disease in some of the actors, but that's almost a given in an Italian horror movie anyway.

The bottom line is that Opera is a joy to watch. Argento's legendary style is captivating as he prowls every inch of the beautiful and impressive opera house in Parma where the movie was shot, and satisfies completely in terms of suspense and gore.

## My Favourite Scene

After realising that she may have unwittingly let the killer into her flat, Betty tries to get to the telephone while her agent goes to the door to see who is out there. As she peers through the peephole, we see her POV as the killer fires a gun, the bullet spinning through the circular chamber before we see a shot of the bullet entering her eye and then exiting through the back of her head.

We then switch to a long shot of the hallway as the bullet slams into a telephone in the foreground, which explodes in a shower of plastic.

Though only a few seconds in duration, there's more imagination and style in this one shot than in the entire running time of some movies.

## Did You Know That

Vanessa Redgrave was originally slated to star in the movie, but dropped out shortly before production began.

Following numerous accidents on set, including the death of one of the actors, Argento believed that the 'Macbeth' curse that is referenced in the movie, and is respected in real theatre life, had struck his production as well.

Actress Daria Nicolodi is the mother of Asia Argento, and has also appeared in many of Dario Argento's movies, including Tenebre, Inferno, Profundo Rosso (aka Deep Red) and Phenomena (aka Creepers). The three have reunited recently to work on Mother of Tears, the concluding part of Argento's long gestating 'Three Mothers' trilogy, of which Suspiria and Inferno are the first two instalments.

# Resident Evil : Apocalypse (2004)

Directed by: Alexander Witt
Written by: Paul W S Anderson
Starring: Milla Jovovich – Alice
Sienna Guillory – Jill Valentine
Oded Fehr – Carlos Olivera
Thomas Kretschmann – Major Cain
Sophie Vavasseur – Angie Anshford

## Synopsis

After surviving a viral outbreak at a secret Umbrella facility called The Hive, Alice finds herself in the middle of an infected Raccoon City, full of the undead. Hooking up with disgraced S.T.A.R.S. operative Jill Valentine and ex-Umbrella soldier Carlos Olivera, Alice attempts to rescue the daughter of a rogue Umbrella scientist and escape from the city before it's too late.

## Why I Love This Movie

Resident Evil came into my life in the summer of 1996 when my friend and fellow gorehound Gary Walters lent me his Playstation for a week while he went on holiday. The reason I had wanted to borrow his newfangled games machine was entirely down to one game, which given the subject of this review is pretty obvious. Yes, Resident Evil had grabbed my attention and held it in a vice like grip as Gary had gleefully showed me several of the save points he had reached, blowning my mind in the process.

Prior to Resident Evil the closest we had come to horror in gaming had been the wonderful Zombies Ate My Neighbours on the Super Nintendo, which while definitely influenced by and paying serious homage to the b-movies that we knew and loved, wasn't actually scary. Dungeon Master on the PC delivered some tense moments, particularly when playing late at night with headphones on, creeping down the claustrophobic corridors and hearing huge spiders scuttling around *somewhere* nearby, but this was nothing compared to the buzz that I felt the first time I ventured into this brave and bloody new world of survival horror.

Quite simply, Resident Evil blew me away. There were zombies, giant spiders, inside-out dogs and even more bizarre creatures, and all set in an old crumbling mansion in the middle of nowhere, complete with secret passages. In short everything a horror movie fan could wish for. Creators Capcom had done their homework and for 1995 were pushing the envelope as to what you could achieve with a horror video game. I played Resident Evil for unhealthy stretches of time, often crawling into my bed in the small hours, and finally finished it, at last able to soothe my ragged throat from all the screams of frustration that had escaped me in the process.

As a result I had high hopes when the first Resident Evil movie came out in 2002. Written and directed by Paul W S Anderson (not to be confused with Paul T Anderson, who directed Boogie Nights and Magnolia) the movie was in the hands of someone who had made a couple of decent movies, most notably 1997's underrated Event Horizon, and who was apparently a huge fan of the series. My only concerns were the fact that traditionally movies based on video games were terrible, and that one of these terrible movies, 1995's Mortal Kombat, was also directed by Anderson.

However, he got it almost right, capturing the atmosphere of the Raccoon City mansion, giving us hordes of zombies, and managing to convincingly pull off the skinned Dobermans without using too much CGI. I had minor niggles, namely that as it was a prequel there were none of the characters from the games, and that thanks to the fast pace those characters we did get weren't fleshed out very much, but these didn't harm my enjoyment of the movie and it would have made it into this book but for one thing. Resident Evil : Apocalypse!

Handing over the directing reins to first timer Alexander Witt, Anderson wisely scripted a movie based around characters and scenes that fans of the games knew and loved, drawing largely on the third game in the series, Resident Evil : Nemesis. Mila Jovovich returned as Alice from the first movie, a welcome addition to the Resident Evil mythology despite not appearing in any of the games or novels, but the trump card was the inclusion of Jill Valentine, heroine of the first and third games and one of my favourite characters from the series.

British actress Sienna Guillory, in her first leading role, brings Jill Valentine perfectly and faithfully to life. The outfit, the attitude, the hair, everything is spot on, even down to the way she stands when waiting for something to happen. Guillory also manages to capture the softer, human side of the ex-S.T.A.R.S. (Special Tactics And Rescue Squad) operative, giving us much more than the one-dimensional characters in the first movie.

Valentine is one uber-cool heroine, and makes her pixellated rival Lara Croft look like an amateur as she punches, kicks and shoots her  way through the infected city with pinpoint accuracy and steely determination.

Jill isn't the only game character who shows up in town, though. Umbrella soldier Carlos Olivera is thrown into the mix, as is the hulking killing machine known as Nemesis (actually a vastly mutated version of one of the characters from the first movie in a nice piece of continuity) who proves to be a worthy, well, nemesis for Alice. Kudos to the makeup department here, as while the Nemesis design looked great in the games, I worried that it would look too static and cheesy in real life, but despite having few facial expressions, this is one very effective monster, and I even find myself feeling some empathy for it.

The main reason that I love this movie is that it looks like it could be a series of cut scenes from the games themselves. From the opening montage, which does a great job of succinctly recounting the events of the first movie in a little over two minutes, there's virtually no let up in the action. Witt manages to convey a feeling of panic and chaos as the citizens of Raccoon City gather on the last open bridge, all other routes having been closed off by the insidious Umbrella corporation to try and contain the outbreak, and are then infiltrated and attacked by the undead. We get shots of the city streets overrun by hordes of walking corpses that are perfectly in tune with the look of the games, and a plethora of impressive set pieces, some of which are lifted almost shot for shot from the series (including my favourite scene from the movie).

This isn't the best action movie ever made, nor is it even close to being the best zombie movie ever made (in fact the zombie action is extremely bloodless considering the source material), but what qualifies this for inclusion is the fact that for ninety minutes it's pure, unadulterated fun. It never sags, the plot is simple enough to prevent any annoying inconsistencies and there are enough quick fire set pieces to satisfy this Resident Evil fan.

In a nod to Lucio Fucli's classic Zombie Flesh Eaters, at one point the main characters find themselves in the middle of a graveyard, and yep, what's a movie about the dead rising without a scene involving them clawing their way out of the ground. Rival horror game Silent Hill gets a nod too in a sequence set in Raccoon City Junior School. We see a map of the world covered in small, bloody hand prints and then the camera pulls back to reveal a gaggle of zombie school children. A quick, but effective and chilling shot.

There's a tense sequence in a church where Jill and her new friends find themselves locked in with a trio of Lickers, the creatures from the second game with tongues that would put KISS's

Gene Simmons to shame, which ends with Alice making a spectacular entrance through a huge stained glass window and taking care of business. Another sequence, one of the most impressive in the movie, has her running down the side of a very tall building at speed to take out the bad guys on the ground. Not to be outdone, however, earlier in the movie Carlos dives out of a helicopter attached to a bungee cord, a gun in each hand in true John Woo style to rescue a woman cornered on the top of another building by the undead.

In a nutshell, this is ninety minutes of action, zombies and most importantly, fun that does exactly what it says on the tin. Definitely a movie made by a Resident Evil fan for Resident Evil fans (despite the inclusion of a token comic relief character that feels tacked on and out of place), this is another of my patented 'two beer' movies – sink a couple of cold ones, park your brain in neutral when you press play and you'll have a blast with this Apocalypse.

## My Favourite Scene

Lifted directly from a cut scene in the Resident Evil : Code Veronica game, towards the end of the movie there is a beautiful shot of Alice running down a circular glass lined corridor, being fired at by a helicopter gunship. As she races along, pursued by the hail of bullets which are shattering the huge windows, raining glass down around her, she rounds a corner to find herself facing three black clad soldiers, their weapons aimed at her.

Apparently surrendering, she lets the gun fall from her hand, but just as it is about to hit the floor she drops, catches it and nails them with three well placed shots. The whole sequence lasts maybe thirty seconds, but Witt's camera work and Anderson's nod to the fans make this scene extremely satisfying.

## Did You Know That...

At the start of the movie a newspaper with the headline 'The Dead Walk' is a homage to a newspaper with an identical headline that appears at the beginning of George A Romero's 1986 Day of the Dead.

Rapper Snoop Dogg was originally chosen to play the role of comic relief LJ, but dropped out and was replaced by Mike Epps

Species actress Natasha Henstridge was originally asked to play Jill Valentine, but couldn't accept the role due to other commitments.

The word 'zombie' is never mentioned in the entire movie.

# Saw (2004)

Directed by:  James Wan
Written by:   Leigh Whannell  (story by James Wan
              and Leigh Whannell)
Starring:     Leigh Whannell – Adam
              Cary Elwes – Dr Lawrence Gordon
              Monica Potter – Alison Gordon
              Danny Glover – Detective David Tapp
              Ken Leung – Detective Steven Sing
              Michael Emmerson – Zep Hindle
              Tobin Bell – Jigsaw

**Synopsis**

Two men awake to find themselves chained to pipes in a
dirty abandoned bathroom, with no idea why they are there.
Slowly but surely it dawns on them that they are the latest victims of a serial killer called Jigsaw whose modus operandi is
setting  up elaborate scenarios and then giving his victims the
opportunity to escape them, but at a terrible price.

**Why I Love This Movie**

Saw is one of those movies that somehow managed to stay
well below my radar until it broke cover, jumping out and pleasantly surprising me with its nastiness. I remember reading about
it in Fangoria just before it was released in October 2004 and
getting that rare but welcome feeling in the pit of my stomach

that something special was brewing. When I finally saw it a few weeks later at the Odeon on Tottenham Court Road in London I was completely blown away by it.

Though not a candidate for this book, one of my favourite movies is David Fincher's much underrated The Game. I love the way that the movie twists and turns, constantly playing with your perceptions of what is happening and always managing to stay one step ahead of any assumptions you make, so when I experienced Saw I was in seventh heaven. Here was a movie that had taken the spirit of Fincher's 1997 masterpiece and grafted it onto a truly horrific premise.

Throughout the movie's duration we are drip fed information and constantly forced to reassess what we already know, or think we know. As each layer of this poisoned onion is peeled back, the plot contorts again and again, but never loses sight of any of the threads that it casts out at the audience. By the time the clever and stunning conclusion comes around, everything makes sense and the pieces of this fiendish jigsaw puzzle have formed a cohesive, if bleak, picture.

Much of Saw's success can be attributed to the two leads, veteran actor Cary Elwes and newcomer, and writer, Leigh Whannell. As the two men who awake to find themselves in a dark, dank, disgusting bathroom with no clue as to why they are there they sell their performances admirably.

Whannell is particularly convincing. His initial confusion as to where the hell he is, followed by panic when he discovers a padlocked chain around his foot, and finally the realisation that he and his fellow prisoner are trapped in similar circumstances and must use their wits to figure out what is going on is utterly believable. I completely bought his character, and for a debut performance, Whannell's turn as Adam is nothing short of superb.

I love the way the two men interact. The dynamic between Elwes and Whannell is priceless. They run the gauntlet from fellow hostages in solidarity to mistrusting enemies and back again thanks to the finely crafted plot that Whannell honed over a five-month period. The fruit of this extended gestation time is reaped in spades. The dialogue is believable and totally consistent with the reactions that you would expect from the two men, particularly as the plot unfolds and we discover that they may not be the strangers they first appear to be.

By giving his own character, Adam, a healthy dose of black humour, Whannell really brings him alive. Being a Brit we often resort to the same kind of dark humour in the direst of situations, so when Adam comes out with these pitch black wise-cracks he scores highly in my book.

For example, when Adam first appraises the situation he finds himself in, the first thing he does is to check his body for scars for fear that the old apocryphal tale of kidney harvesters has become a reality. Later, when one of Jigsaw's riddles suggests that something vital to understanding their situation is hidden in a toilet next to Adam, he thrusts his hand deep into the filthy bowl, finding nothing, before checking the cistern and discovering the hidden prize, declaring "I wish I'd checked in there first." There are no Schwarzenneger-style quips or knowing asides to the camera in Saw, just dialogue that feels genuine and natural given the circumstances.

Elwes's character, Doctor Lawrence Gordon, is the perfect foil for Adam. His reactions are measured and controlled, as befits the manner of a surgeon, whereas Adam's are manic and kinetic. Throughout the movie he somehow manages to remain in control of himself, even knowing that his wife and daughter are in grave danger, so when he finally snaps, under circumstances that are completely plausible, it is a shocking contrast to the Lawrence that we have come to know.

The real star of the show, however, as is often the case with a great Saturday Night Fright Flick, is the villain. Jigsaw is a departure from the traditional psychopaths that usually plan elaborate ruses in a couple of vital ways. The first major difference is that while his modus operandi is both clever and sadistic, his actual motive is actually noble and understandable. Having had his destiny taken out of his hands, he seeks to make others realise just how precious their lives are and attempts to show them the error of their ways.

Jigsaw is no soulless serial killer, no Freddy Krueger or Michael Myers, but rather he reminds me of Se7en's John Doe, another villain who believes he is doing good work. As much as I love Michael, Jason and Fred, for me the most chilling psychopaths are those who are firmly grounded in reality. Maniacs like Buffalo Bill, the deranged dressmaker from Jonathan Demme's 1991 classic The Silence of the Lambs, or Terry O'Quinn's marvellous portrayal of The Stepfather really work for me. There are no supernatural elements at play with these guys, and they could quite literally live next door to you.

Tobin Bell's Jigsaw is similarly intriguing. For the vast majority of the film we don't even see him, though his presence is felt in almost every scene, in more ways than one for those who have previously seen the movie or are particularly perceptive, but when we hear him speak, usually via the handheld tape recorders that he is so fond of, his voice is captivating. He reminds me of a more measured and rational version of Fred Krueger, but without the wise cracks. Every word is spoken with purpose and you can't help but listen intently to him, just as the players in his twisted games are forced to do in order to have any hope of surviving them.

This brings me to my absolute favourite thing about Saw - the games themselves. Writer Whannell's imagination was clearly in overdrive when he conceived the elaborate scenarios that his victims find themselves in. The first victim we are introduced to, a man who has recently attempted suicide, has been given the choice of remaining locked in a room to die or escaping by crawling through a trap full of razor wire. The second is a man who is smeared with a flammable substance, injected with a slow acting poison and told that the antidote is in the locked safe in the room with him. The catch is that the room is dark, the safe's combination is written on the walls, and he has only a candle to see the numbers by. Oh, and the floor is covered in broken glass.

Jigsaw may want his victims to do the right thing and survive so that they may learn from their experience, but you can't help but smile at the sadistic hoops he makes them jump through in order to achieve this goal. To top it all he is the ultimate voyeur, liking to watch his games play out from close quarters. A sick puppy for sure, but one of the most imaginative, smart and entertaining psychos that I've come across in many years.

Saw is quite simply a great rollercoaster of a movie. A slow burning ride, granted, but one that never lets up the intensity for a minute, constantly revealing more and more layers until the movie's ultimate pay-off in the dying minutes. When I first saw it in the darkened confines of the Odeon a huge grin broke out across my face at the sheer audacity of the ending. Again drawing parallels to The Game, it's an ending you will either love or hate, but I personally thought it was the cleverest twist that I'd seen for a long time, and it still makes me grin like a lunatic.

In short, a great Saturday Night Fright Flick. Well written and crammed full of quality performances, particularly Danny Glover's turn as Detective Tapp, a cop who is a million miles away from the more familiar territory of Lethal Weapon's Roger Murtaugh as he relentlessly pursues his obsession with catching Jigsaw. Saw proves that there are still filmmakers out there, along with the likes of Rob Zombie and Eli Roth, who are committed to returning our beloved genre to its blood soaked roots and leaving the crop of, admittedly entertaining at times, PG-13 horror movies in their dust.

**My Favourite Scene**

The 'reverse bear trap' scene with Shawnee Smith's character Amanda. This is the first time we see one of Jigsaw's games actually in motion, and is my favourite of all of them.

Amanda comes to, tied to a chair with a huge metal contraption strapped to her head. A monitor next to her comes to life and Jigsaw's evil puppet tells her that the device is locked, but that the key is located in the stomach of a body lying across the room from her. He explains that the device works on a timer and shows her, with the aid of a plaster head, exactly what is about to happen to her.

She panics, freeing herself from her bindings and stands up, only to have Jigsaw pull one of his twists. By standing up she has pulled the pin on the timer and it is only now that the countdown begins. Terrified, she reaches the body, and with the scalpel that Jigsaw has thoughtfully left nearby is about to cut into the stomach when he pulls another twist. The supposedly dead body's eyes open!

This is an intense and horrific sequence that perfectly captures the spirit of what Saw is all about.

## Did You Know That...

Wan and Whannell filmed a ten-minute short of the reverse bear trap sequence, with Whannell in the role of Amanda, to act as a calling card along with the script. It worked.

The scene in which Whannell's character thrusts his hand into the dirty toilet bowl is an homage to Danny Boyle's 1996 movie Trainspotting.

The entire movie was shot in a converted warehouse studio. Of the sets, only the bathroom was purpose built, with all the others being redressed existing locations at the studio.

The creepy puppet that Jigsaw uses is an homage to a similar one in Dario Argento's 1975 classic Profundo Rosso (aka Deep Red).

Leigh Whannell asked for Shawnee Smith to be approached for the role of Amanda as a joke, having had a crush on her for years. He never expected her to even consider the role and was completely, but pleasantly, surprised when she signed up.

# Scream (1996)

Directed by:   Wes Craven
Written by:   Kevin Williamson
Starring:   Neve Campbell – Sidney Prescott
                Courteney Cox – Gail Weathers
                David Arquette – Deputy 'Dewey' Riley
                Skeet Ulrich – Billy Loomis
                Matthew Lillard – Stuart Macher
                Rose McGowan – Tatum Riley
                Jamie Kennedy – Randy Meeks
                Drew Barrymore – Casey Becker

**Synopsis**

Two teens are brutally slain in the small town of Woodsboro by a psychopath who is well versed in the rules of horror movies.

Meanwhile student Sidney Prescott is dealing with the murder of her mother the previous year, but after being contacted by the killer begins to suspect that she may have helped to convict the wrong man.

As the body count starts to climb, the police and Sidney's friends attempt to identify the killer, but find that they nearly all have motives that could place them in the killer's boots.

## Why I Love This Movie

By 1996 the horror movie genre was on its knees. Certainly in the United Kingdom there were precious few flicks that actually got a cinema release, and those that did were largely unremarkable, rehashing the same tired old clichés that had been the backbone of the genre since the 1980s.

Sure, there had been the occasional diamond in the rough, like Jonathan Demme's superb 1991 classic The Silence of the Lambs, but even that was touted as a psychological thriller, the term 'horror movie' having become a dirty word in marketing circles, and the kiss of death for the all important box office returns.

It's something of an understatement, then, to say that when genre legend Wes Craven, the man behind the infamous Last House on the Left and The Hills Have Eyes, and the father of bastard son of a hundred maniacs Freddy Krueger, announced that he was working on something that would revolutionise and revive the genre, I was more than a little excited.

I was also apprehensive, however, as while Craven was, and is, undeniably a master of his craft, it had been a few years since he had produced anything of note, and he was working from a script, provisionally titled 'Wes Craven's Scary Movie', by an unknown scribe called Kevin Williamson. In retrospect I needn't have worried, as the partnering of these two creative forces created a synergy, and a movie, that has resonated throughout the genre ever since and did indeed reanimate it to a degree that even more than a decade later there is still a healthy crop of theatrical horror releases each year.

Inevitably, as was the case during the last genre boom in the 1980s, they aren't all great movies, and some stink worse than the inside of Jason's mask, but at least as horror fans we're getting the opportunity to see them where they belong, on the big screen.

What I love about Craven's Scream trilogy is the fact that Williamson wasn't afraid to take the accepted rules of horror movies, more of which later, and acknowledge that the teens we were watching on screen weren't the usual hapless victims that we were used to, but were in fact very well versed, thanks largely to Jamie Kennedy's loveable movie geek Randy, in the real world of horror movies.

As Neve Campbell's character Sidney tells the killer on the phone, she doesn't watch scary movies because it's always "Some stupid killer stalking some big breasted girl who can't act, who's always running up the stairs when she should be going out the front door. It's insulting." Randy follows up this nodding wink to the audience later on by distilling the lessons learned from previous horror movies into three easy rules:

Rule 1:    You can never have sex.
Rule 2:    You can never drink or do drugs.
Rule 3:    Never, ever, ever under any circumstances
           say 'I'll be right back'.

As a genre fan these observations hit the bulls-eye. Looking back at the old 1980s classics like Halloween or Friday the 13th, or any number of the pale imitations that followed them, you can pretty much pick the victims and the survivors out in the first ten minutes of the movies. The characters could be ticked off on your I-Spy chart of horror movies – Slut? Check. Stoner? Check. Virginal good girl? Check. Supportive but ultimately doomed boyfriend of said virginal good girl? Check.

Most of these old school horror teens were utterly disposable and as John Cleese's Mr Creosote might remark, 'wafer thin', but Scream's great advantage and one of its strongest calling cards was the sheer depth and believability of Kevin Williamson's characters. There isn't a single character in Scream that comes across as clichéd (except where the cliché is played for deliberate irony) or surplus to requirements.

In fact I was so impressed by Williamson's writing, after which he completed his genre hat-trick with 1997's I Know What You Did Last Summer and 1998's The Faculty, that I actually found myself watching the first two seasons of his teen drama series Dawson's Creek on the strength of his name alone. It didn't hurt that Katie Holmes and Michelle Williams, both of whom subsequently carved out decent careers, were very easy on the eye, but the quality of the writing and the authentic feel of the characters kept me coming back for more.

Another thing that, for me, worked so well in Scream's favour was the decision to cast relatively unknown actors in the teen leads. Neve Campbell, previously known for her work in another teen TV drama, Party of Five, works well as Sidney Prescott, making us believe in her ongoing struggle to deal with her mother's murder and the fact that she may not have been the saint that Sidney wants to believe she was. This emotional vulnerability is superbly juxtaposed with her fighting spirit. This shines through when she calls the killer's bluff during a conversation in which he tells her that he is outside her front door, promptin her to defiantly open it and step out onto the porch to confront him, and when she punches reporter Gail Weathers in the face during a confrontation outside the police station.

Skeet Ulrich, as Sidney's boyfriend Billy Loomis (a nod to Donald Pleasance's character Dr Sam Loomis in John Carpenter's 1980 classic Halloween), comes across as a younger version of Johnny Depp (never a bad thing), and adeptly handles the script's need for him to alternately have us believe that he may or may not be the killer. Craven, obviously acknowledging the resemblance, even replicates a shot of Depp climbing into Heather Langencamp's bedroom in A Nightmare On Elm Street, when Billy climbs in through Sidney's window.

Rose McGowan, one time squeeze of Marilyn Manson, provides a feisty and trusted best friend to Sidney, but also one of the more inventive exits from a movie that I'd seen for a while, and Matthew Lillard is perfect cast as her crass, overbearing and tactless boyfriend Stu. The banter between Lillard and Ulrich veers between affection and complete disdain for each other, but is always entertaining.

My favourite of the teens, though, is Randy. Jamie Kennedy's movie geek with a bottomless pit of genre knowledge is worth the price of admission alone. Whether suggesting that the police could save some time in their investigation by watching Prom Night, educating the audience about the rules of horror movies, or officially affirming Jamie Leigh Curtis's legendary Scream Queen status after Sidney asks why she is in The Fog, Terror Train *and* Prom Night, Randy makes me smile because he *is* the horror movie geek that lives in all of us.

Of the 'grown ups', Courtney Cox is very entertaining as hard-nosed, ruthless TV anchor-woman Gail Weathers, proving to the world that there is more to her than Monica Gellar, but it is David Arquette who really shines as Deputy Dwight 'Dewey' Riley. Clearly good at his job, having risen to the rank of Deputy at the ripe old age of twenty-five, he can't shake the public's perception of him as Woodsboro's very own Keystone Kop. When his sister Tatum calls him Dewey in the squad room he visibly rankles and reminds her "What did mum tell you? When I wear this badge you treat me like a man of the law", drawing sniggers and laughs from the rest of the squad room. You can't help but warm to the man in the same way that you'd warm to a puppy that keeps falling over his own feet.

The thing I love most about Scream, though, is the unashamed way in which it pays respect to its roots. For the genre fan there are so many in jokes and references to pick up on, from the trick question about the killer in the original Friday the 13th during Drew Barrymore's opening telephone odreal, to the brief cameos by Linda Blair as a reporter and Wes Craven himself as a red and green sweater wearing janitor called Fred; from Tatum's comment to Sidney that "you're starting to sound like some Wes Carpenter flick", to Mr Becker's instructions to his wife to "Drive down to the Mackenzie's".

In retrospect, Scream was exactly what both the genre and the fans needed at that point in time, and was a shot in the arm that continues to be felt even now. It also gave me one of my all time favourite quotes from any movie, and one which I find myself using on the occasions where I have to defend my love of all things red - "Don't blame the movies. Movies don't create psychos. Movies make psychos more creative." Perfect Saturday Night Fright Flick material and an essential part of anyone's collection.

## My Favourite Scene

The opening twelve minutes of Scream are a master class in how to create tension, and then maintain it before delivering a left-field twist that I confess I didn't see coming.

Preparing for an evening watching a horror movie with her boyfriend, Drew Barrymore's character Casey Becker receives a phone call from a man who initially seems to have a wrong number. He calls again and flirts with her but she isn't interested and hangs up. He calls back a third time and they begin to talk, engaging in light hearted banter until he asks her name. She asks why he wants to know to which he replies that he wants to know who he's looking at.

At this point the mood turns ugly and Craven slowly tightens the terror thumbscrews as Casey becomes more scared and hysterical, particularly when the killer reveals that he has her boyfriend Steve tied to a chair on the patio. He insists that they play a game for Steve's life and asks her questions about horror movies. She gets the answers to the first one right but then he throws her a curve ball that anyone but diehard genre fans would easily be tripped up on. She gets it wrong and, as promised, Steve is gutted like a fish.

The killer then comes after her and a chase through the house ensues before Casey heads out into the garden, running for her life. He catches her just as her parents pull up and Craven cruelly allows her to stagger towards them, gasping but unable to speak, just yards away from them as they enter the house. Her mother picks up the phone and hears Casey being stabbed again and then dragged away. She runs out into the yard to find Casey hanging from a tree.

This opening scene was a bold move for Craven, not only because it goes on for twelve minutes and never once sags or loses momentum, but because he had the audacity to kill off a major star at the top of the movie, something that hadn't been seen in a major horror movie since Janet Leigh was offed in the first reel of Alfred Hitchcock's 1960 masterpiece Psycho.

**Did You Know That...**

In order to keep Drew Barrymore looking scared during the opening sequence, Wes Craven kept telling her real life stories of animal cruelty, knowing that they would upset her.

Sabrina The Teenage Witch (aka Melissa Joan Hart) and Charmed's Piper (aka Neve Campbell look-a-like Holly Marie Combs) both auditioned for the role of Sidney Prescott.

Tatum (Rose McGowan) wears a football jersey style top with the number 10 on it, a nod to the one worn by Johnny Depp in Craven's 1984 A Nightmare On Elm Street.

Close to fifty gallons of blood were used during the making of Scream.

The house used for the opening sequence was situated next door to the one used in Lewis Teague's 1983 adaptation of Stephen King's rabid dog tale Cujo.

# Se7en (1995)

Directed by:    David Fincher
Written by:     Andrew Kevin Walker
Starring:       Brad Pitt – Detective David Mills
                Morgan  Freeman
                            – Detective William Somerset
                Gwyneth Paltrow – Tracy Mills
                Kevin Spacey – John Doe
                R Lee Ermey – Police Captain

## Synopsis

A psychopath is killing his victims in the manner of the seven deadly sins. Veteran cop Somerset and his cynical young partner Mills attempt to track him down with little success when suddenly the cat and mouse game is turned on its head.

As the killer plays with their minds his plan hurtles towards its unexpected and shocking conclusion.

## Why I Love This Movie

Se7en was one of those rare movies that became a huge hit despite attracting very little press before it was released, largely due to the fact that director David Fincher wasn't the household name that he has become today. Having been unfairly slated for his third entry in the Alien series, I personally thought that 1992's Alien3 wasn't anywhere as bad as the reviews suggested. In fact, having seen the extended work print included in the

Alien Quadrilogy box set, I think it's very nearly as good as Ridley Scott and James Cameron's previous entries in the franchise, and a million times better than Jean-Pierre Jeunet's unnecessary and unsatisfying Alien Resurrection.

Se7en unwittingly benefited from being one of the last generation of movies that came out before the rise of the internet, and so was one of the last great movies to experience good old fashioned word of mouth promotion. As a genre fan I was already aware of Se7en and saw it on the opening weekend, but it was fascinating to watch the whole 'what's in the box' speculation spread like wildfire among people who only rarely darkened the doorways of their local cinema, and then listen to their thoughts on the ending, which certainly took me by surprise.

Se7en also had the distinction of being the last great horror movie before the onslaught of the whole 'ironic' genre that kicked off the following year with Wes Craven's iconic Scream, which changed the landscape for a good few years and is still felt as an influence on today's genre offerings. As a consequence Fincher wasn't afraid to deliver a genuinely chilling and bleak movie, without a single funny quip or knowing glance to the camera.

I love the relentlessly miserable and downbeat feel that infuses Se7en, and that the city, which is never named and thus has the feel of Anytown, USA, is constantly lashed with rain, giving the locations a dark and dank feel which perfectly echo Somerset's supposed reasons for wanting to retire. He tells his Captain, played by the always fantastic R Lee Ermey, that he "doesn't understand this place any more" and later explains to Mills that he "cannot continue to live in a place that nurtures apathy as a virtue."

While on paper Se7en might appear to be nothing more than just another cop buddy movie with its pairing of the retiring Somerset and the enthusiastic and idealistic young Mills, in the capable hands of Fincher and writer Andrew Kevin Walker, who went on to score a double whammy in 1999 with the underrated Nic Cage thriller 8MM and Johnny Depp's eccentric turn as Ichabod Crane in Tim Burton's Sleepy Hollow, Se7en is elevated to a much higher plane.

The interaction between the two men is fascinating to watch, as their two very different world views collide. Somerset is a thinker, and has garnered a reputation as such over the years, preferring to use his mind and logic as his weapons in the fight against crime, rather than his gun, which in his thirty-four years on the job he has never fired in the line of duty. When researching the seven deadly sins in a wonderfully ornate library he tells the security guards there that he can't understand why, with so much knowledge surrounding them, they instead choose to play poker.

His disillusion with the world is the compete antithesis of the verve and energy with which Mills attacks the case. Somerset recognises his need to be a champion, to save the world, and tries to tell him that people don't want champions, but Mills is undeterred and instead, as the two men become more comfortable with each other as the week that the movie encompasses progresses, tries to convince Somerset that he is retiring for the wrong reasons, and that he wants Mills to confirm his nihilistic world view, which of course he won't.

Somerset is the methodical mentor to the impulsive and impatient Mills, and Freeman and Pitt have such chemistry on screen together that the characters are completely believable as they make the transition from strangers to friends over the course of the week, gradually earning each others trust and respect.

Gwyneth Paltrow pulls off a fine performance as Mills' wife Tracy who initially acts as the bridge between the two men, and later becomes a pivotal piece of the puzzle as she confides in Somerset and then, well, if you've seen the movie you know what, and if you haven't then you really should at the earliest opportunity. Like right now.

The real acting kudos in this movie, though, go to Kevin Spacey, who puts in a career best performance as John Doe. When I saw Se7en at the cinema my jaw dropped when he finally steps from the shadows at the top of the final reel in one of the most unexpected twists to ever grace a horror movie. Of the many maniacs and serial killers that have stalked their way across the screen over the years, few have chilled me quite as much as John Doe.

It is the sheer ordinariness of the man that makes him so unnerving. Delivering his twisted logic in a calm, measured, almost monotone voice he utterly mesmerises the audience, and even now after seeing Se7en many times I find myself riveted to the screen watching Spacey's performance. John Doe is a frighteningly intelligent and patient man, showing no emotion, no fear, and no remorse, and this makes him positively terrifying.

The intelligence and originality behind his crimes elevates Se7en above being just another serial killer of the week movie. Walker crafted a script that is brave enough to credit the audience with some intelligence as it slowly reveals John Doe's work, rather than the, unfortunately, more usual route of spoon feeding the viewer every step of the way.

Regarding the seven deadly sins themselves, Fincher cleverly allows much of it to be seen only after the fact, leaving us to fill in the blanks with images far more horrific than anything we could be shown on screen. The murder scenes reminded me of the stylistic opening of John McNaughton's Henry : Portrait Of A Serial Killer in which he pans across several grisly murder scenes some time after the crime has occurred but plays the soundtrack of the actual murders over the top. Chilling stuff, given a fresh lease of life by Fincher in Se7en.

When we see the first victim, hog tied with barbed wire and force fed to bursting point, we don't need to have seen the actual crime itself. The grisly tableau that we walk in on tells the story more graphically than seeing it played out ever could.

Likewise the extremely effective way Fincher handles the lust murder. We are briefly shown a Polaroid picture of the weapon, and then the hysterical ramblings of the reluctant proxy murderer whose emotional aftershocks resonate far deeper and longer than if we'd seen the actual crime itself.

Se7en is one of those rare movies that combines a top-notch cast with an intelligent and well written script, putting it in such distinguished company as Jonathan Demme's Oscar wining Silence Of The Lambs, but what transcends even these credentials to firmly cement it as one of my all time favourite movies is the ending.

Thanks to Fincher having the balls to stick his guns, allegedly with Pitt's support and backing, he demanded that the studio go with the bleaker of two proposed endings and in doing so elevated the final minutes of the movie into history as one of those finales that people will talk about forever. I personally love the dark tone of the endgame which echoes reality in that it acknowledges that situations like the one Somerset and Mills find themselves in rarely turn out well in real life.

I never tire of this movie. Though I know it inside out, it's like putting on a favourite album. I know the beats and the rhythms and still, every time, I am entranced by it. Se7en is not just one of my favourite horror flicks of all time, but one of my favourite flicks full stop. Panic Room aside, which was good but not great, Fincher has yet to put a foot wrong in my eyes. If you've never seen Se7en, do so this Saturday, and if you have then you don't need me to tell you how close to perfection this movie is.

**My Favourite Scene**

What could it be except those final few minutes as John Doe finally reveals the sheer brilliance of his plan. Mills and Somerset have walked willingly into his carefully orchestrated finale and he has cleverly allowed them to believe that they have the upper hand. Until the box arrives, that is.

At this point the tension becomes unbearable as Mills falls deeper into his trap and Somerset desperately tries to pull him out of it. Even after repeated viewings my nerves fray watching Mills tip over the edge of sanity and reason. One of cinema's all time great endings.

**Did You Know That...**

All the building numbers in the opening scene begin with 7, and the final delivery is scheduled for 7:07pm.

The Gluttony victim is actually writer Andrew Kevin Walker in heavy (literally) makeup.

Denzel Washington was originally offered the part of Mills, and R.E.M. singer Michael Stipe was considered for the role of John Doe.

All of the notebooks in John Doe's apartment were real, and were handwritten specifically for the film. The time taken to produce these books, two months, is the same amount of time that Somerset estimates that it would take to read them all.

Kevin Spacey was originally intended to be the top billing in the movie, but insisted that his name be excluded from the opening credits so as to surprise the audience when John Doe's identity is finally revealed. As compensation he is listed first in the end credits.

Despite his horrific crimes, John Doe is never seen to kill anyone on screen.

When shown on terrestrial television in the United Kingdom, among the cuts made are the inexplicable removal of the Polaroid of the lust murder weapon, the absence of which makes the whole scene unfathomable to those who aren't aware of what has happened.

# The Stepfather (1987)

Directed by:   Joseph Ruben
Written by:    Donald E Westlake, Brian Garfield and
               Carolyn Lefcourt
Starring:      Terry O'Quinn – Jerry Blake
               Jill Schloen – Stephanie Maine
               Shelly Hack – Susan Maine
               Charles Lanyer – Dr Bondurant
               Stephen Sheelen – Jim Ogilvie

**Synopsis**

Jerry Blake always wanted the perfect family, so when he marries a beautiful widow and becomes Stepfather to her lovely daughter he appears to have found it. Again.

When they begin to disappoint him, however, not living up to his expectations of what constitutes the perfect family, he is willing to go to any lengths to protect his ideals and keep the family together.

**Why I Love This Movie**

Throughout the 1980s I couldn't get enough of the wealth of schlock horror movies that were churned out as the popularity of the genre exploded in the wake of films like A Nightmare On Elm Street. Wes Craven's 1984 classic brought horror to the masses and in true capitalist style, if something works then the market will replicate it to death.

Thankfully my local video store was crammed to capacity with an ever-increasing library of crappy horror movies. Street Trash, The Stuff, C.H.U.D., Scarecrows and a thousand others passed across the heads of my video recorder, most of which were virtually forgotten as soon as I'd put them back in the box. Occasionally, though, a real gem would shine out of the ever-increasing mountain of gargage. The Stepfather was one of these diamonds.

As I've noted before, I love horror movies that bring maniacs right into the safe, all-American confines of Anywhere, USA. Halloween and A Nightmare On Elm Street are arguably the most famous movies to have done this, inflicting Michael Myers and Fred Krueger onto their respective communities, but both of these villains had an element of the supernatural about them.

Jerry Blake, the titular Stepfather, however, is just a normal, flesh and blood man who could literally live next door. OK, so normal isn't quite the word, given his habit of slaughtering the families that don't live up to his strict ideals of the perfect unit, but there is nothing remotely powered up or extraordinary about him. He's just a tad insane, is all.

What really sells this movie for me is Terry O'Quinn's performance as Blake. Like William H Macy, O'Quinn is one of those great character actors who is utterly convincing in whatever role he inhabits, particularly when there's a hint of darkness to it. This was very much the case in his recurring role as Peter Watts on the short-lived but compelling Millennium series, where he played the head of a mysterious underground investigative group, and in his highest profile role to date, as John Locke in the ongoing Lost series.

From the first moment we see him, heavily bearded and covered in gore, there isn't a shadow of a doubt that this man is several sandwiches short of a picnic. O'Quinn has this wonderful look that is part boredom, part bemusement and part pure, unadulterated mania, and he uses it frequently, to devastating effect. He puts in a performance that is a knife edge away from being over-the-top but somehow manages not to tip over the edge into parody.

There are two vital ingredients that no self respecting eighties horror movie would be caught dead without. The first is the legacy of the second Nightmare On Elm Street movie, 1985's somewhat lame Freddy's Revenge, which managed to take the genuinely scary supernatural child killer of the first movie and turn him into a comedian. Henceforth it became *de rigueur* for horror villains to indulge in a bout of wise cracking as they laid waste to their victims. Not wanting to be left out, Blake lets loose with a few choice quips, the best, or worst depending on your point of view, coming as he straps his latest victim into the front seat of his car and deadpans 'buckle up for safety'.

The second is that most essential of shots for an eighties slasher movie, the gratuitous tit shot. It seemed that back in the day sooner or later one or more nubile young girls would end up stripping off to either have sex with their boyfriends (and occasionally each other), thus signing their death warrants as the masked killer *du jour* bumped them off shortly thereafter, or to climb into the shower and proceed to work themselves and the audience into a lather.

Not all shower scenes were gratuitous, though. The one at the beginning of Carrie actually served a purpose in the plot (although Brian De Palma was no stranger to the gratuitous nude scene, as witnessed by his 1984 sleaze fest Body Double), and Janet Leigh's premature demise in the granddaddy of them all, Hitchcock's classic Psycho, wouldn't have been half as effective set anywhere else (though, granted, there was no explicit nudity).

True to form, late on in the movie, just at the point when she really should not be getting naked and vulnerable, stepdaughter Stephanie strips off for a completely unnecessary shower, flashing her breasts at us in the process, although this does feel somewhat voyeuristic in a creepy way as we have recently been told that she's only just turned sixteen (although in real life actress Jill Schloen was twenty-four when she shot the movie). The

Stepfather can't be accused of sexism, though, as Terry O'Quinn strips off for his own shower scene at the top of the movie, and even flashes us a brief full frontal shot.

The Stepfather's great strength, and the reason that I love this movie, is that from the very start we are under no illusion as to who is the lunatic here (though to be fair, I suppose the title kind of gives it away), so there's no tedious 'who is the killer' detective element, only the delicious anticipation of when Blake is going to lose it and who is going to be on the receiving end when he does. Thanks to the brother of his most recent victim being on the case, we get Blake's modus operandi drip fed to us, and so when history begins to repeat itself, we know that we've just crested the last hill on this roller coaster ride and we're into the home straight. Good news for us, but not for Blake's latest family.

There's a great sequence in the basement of the house, where Blake has fled to after reading a story about his previous exploits in the local paper, as we watch him pacing up and down, throwing things about and muttering to himself, all the time being watched by a terrified Stephanie who has come down to get some ice.

He appears to be having a conversation with himself ('you are going to keep this family together', 'you better believe it') which stirs echoes of Norman Bates, and true to psycho killer form he needs a back story, which from the not so cryptic clues that he gives us during the movie seems to stem from a bad childhood. Now there's a surprise. O'Quinn pulls off this schizophrenia magnificently and always puts a smile on my face when I watch this. Though not as technically brilliant as Willem Dafoe's turn as Norman Osborne in Spider-man (what *is* it with Normans and schizophrenia?) or Andy Serkis's superb portrayal of Gollum's madness in Lord of the Rings: Return of the King, O'Quinn plays the everyman nutcase to perfection.

Overall, The Stepfather works primarily thanks to O'Quinn, but also because of a reasonably intelligent script. Some thought has clearly gone into the plot and pacing, and this shows. Never dull and not afraid to embrace the violence and gore (unlike the crop of PG-13 movies that plagued the genre in the wake of Scream), The Stepfather is ninety minutes of pure schlock horror entertainment, and even produced a decent sequel, Stepfather II, again starring O'Quinn.

## My Favourite Scene

After cleaning himself up following his latest bout of handi-work, Blake shaves, puts on fresh clothes and makes his way through the immaculately kept house to the stairs. There are pictures of the happy family on the walls, and this seems like the perfect suburban family home.

As he descends, however, we notice first a bloody handprint on the wall, a thick trail of red leading down, and then as he reaches the foot of the stairs, we see that the downstairs of the house is completely trashed. Furniture is overturned, pictures are smashed and lying in amongst this destruction are the bodies of his now ex-wife and son.

This brief transition from the apparently normal upper level of the house to the chaotic and bloody ground floor serves as analogy for the perfect family descending into hell, and of the two very different planes of Blake's mind, both of which he is completely comfortable in. A visually striking scene, and one that sets the tone for the rest of the movie.

## Did You Know That...

There was a second sequel, 1992's Stepfather III starring Robert Wightman as the now surgically altered psycho. Wightman had previously played John-Boy Walton Jr in several episodes of The Waltons

Terry O'Quinn is a talented guitarist and singer, and can apparently do a very accurate impression of Neil Young.

# The Texas Chain Saw Massacre (1974)

Directed by: Tobe Hooper
Written by: Kim Henkel and Tobe Hooper
Starring: Marilyn Burns – Sally Hardesty
Paul A Partain – Franklin Hardesty
Allen Danziger – Jerry
William Vail – Kirk
Teri McMinn – Pam
Edwin Neal – The Hitchhiker
Jim Seidow – Old Man
Gunnar Hansen – Leatherface
John Dugan – Grandfather Sawyer

**Synopsis**

Five twenty-somethings are on a road trip to make sure that the grave of Sally and Franklin Hardesty's grandfather hasn't been disturbed following news reports of recent desecrations. After picking up a hitchhiker who uses a knife to cut first himself and then Franklin, they throw him out of the van and speed away in disgust.

Stopping at a gas station they are informed that the tanks are dry but that a delivery is due that afternoon. To kill time they drive up to their grandfather's old place while waiting for the tanker. Before long they discover that his neighbours are a family of dysfunctional cannibals who are more than happy to take advantage of the fresh supply of meat.

## Why I Love This Movie

In 1982 some friends of my parents who lived two doors down from us had just bought one of these new-fangled video recorder things. Their three teenage sons, who were a few years older than me, had subsequently discovered the delights of the horror section of the local video shop and were working their way through it.

Graham, their father, had mentioned this to my Mum one night while they were at the local pub and she in turn had told him of my love of horror movies. Graham then told her that they had rented some movie called The Texas Chain Saw Massacre and were going to watch it the following afternoon, and that I was welcome to come over and join them.

So, that Sunday afternoon after we had finished our roast dinner, I found myself sititng on the sofa in the Ballham's house with Mark, Simon and Adrian, to watch this movie that I hadn't heard of at this point, but which rumour had it was apparently the most horrific and depraved experience ever committed to celluloid.

From the opening shots of the desecrated Texan graveyard to Leatherface's lunatic dance in the highway some eighty minutes later I was entranced. I had never seen a movie that was so intense, so relentless and though, at 12 years old I was only beginning to come to terms with the concept, so downright sadistic in its treatment of the victims.

The initial brief glimpses of decaying body parts illuminated by a flash gun and accompanied by one of the most unique and recognisable sounds in horror movies, are extremely powerful and strangely beautiful, in a macabre way. Director Tobe Hooper cuts to a close up of a leering skull, which as he pulls the camera back we discover is part of a tableaux of two bodies wired to a gravestone. This shot, with the big, bright Texas sun in the background lingers for just over a minute and is still every bit as potent and unsettling now as it was the first time I saw it.

From the outset Hooper populates his movie with wonderful visuals which continue throughout, infusing the scenery and sets with as much life as the characters themselves, if not more. When the friends pull over to pick up a hitchhiker, Hooper fills the screen with the bright Texas sky, the van merely a small detail crawling across the bottom of the frame like an insect on a windowsill.

Hooper further captures the feelings of isolation and menace that pervade the first half of the movie by using a sparse soundtrack that relies largely on natural sounds such as the constant drone of the engine and the conversation of the characters. This is accentuated only by a radio show playing blues songs faintly in the background, punctuated by frequent news bulletins describing all manner of horrific events, including the desecration of the graveyard that we saw at the top of the movie.

Though they have since become stereotypical characters, when TCM first came out, and even when I first saw it eight years later, the five friends were reasonably accurate portrayals of their generation's youth. None of them are particularly appealing people, the four able-bodied friends often leaving the wheelchair bound Franklin to struggle along for himself while they explore the area, not that we feel much sympathy for him either, as he moans and complains and whines. However, they all feel realistic and like the kind of group that genuinely would be hanging out together, rather than the stereotypical mix-and-match teen groups that populated the 1990s teen slasher movies.

The movie's real stars, though, are the Sawyer family, probably one of my all time favourite dysfunctional families. Edwin Neal's Hitchhiker is wonderfully underplayed, appearing on the surface to be just another of those weird guys that you'd cross the street to avoid, but once we get to know him a little when he's in the van it becomes obvious that beneath this needy, almost pathetic puppy dog exterior is a man whose elevator doesn't quite reach the top floor, and in fact may well have stalled some way down the shaft.

The most normal (and I use the term relatively here) of the three active Sawyer boys, not counting the largely inanimate and practically mummified Grandfather, is Jim Seidow's character, referred to only as the Old Man in the credits. He initially appears to be the voice of reason in the family, a father figure almost, as he berates the other two for effectively playing with their food when they torment Sally later in the movie. However, we soon find out that although, by his own admission, he "just can't take no pleasure in killing", he isn't averse to a little sadistic torment himself. He beats Sally with a broom to subdue her after apparently rescuing her, and then prods her with a stick as she cowers in the footwell of his truck, tied and gagged, telling her with a leering grin, "I hope you're not too uncomfortable down there."

It is Leatherface, though, who remains indelibly burned on the memory long after the credits have rolled. One of my favourite movie villains, right up there with Freddy, Jason and Michael in the horror hall of fame, Leatherface is one of the more unlikely movie psychos. Unlike the other three, who are cold, emotionless killing machines, Junior is a truly pathetic soul. Bullied by his brothers, subservient to the point of doing housework dressed in a variety of dead skin masks and generally considered even by his family to be an idiotic halfwit, Leatherface truly comes alive when he picks up his chainsaw and becomes that most dangerous of psychopaths, those who kill for the sheer pleasure of it.

Whether carving up a body in his workshop or chasing Sally through the woods, I love that Bubba seems to actually be enjoying it, squealing like a pig as he carries out his work. Gunnar Hansen breathes real life into Leatherface, more than compensating for the lack of vocalisation, save for the squeals, by accentuating his body movements and making us believe that this is a jumpy, skittish, mentally challenged young man. When shouted at by his brothers he visibly flinches, and even as he goes about chasing and killing his victims there is a certain innocence to it, as though even though what he is doing is horrific, he

146

doesn't know any better and is only doing what comes naturally to him.

My absolute favourite thing about this movie, though, is the same thing that earned it such a reputation, and indeed an effective ban in the UK for many years. The sheer intensity that Hooper infuses into this film is incredible. This is not a movie that you can watch passively. Hooper drags you into the intense atmosphere, and creates scenes of such length that it drains you to watch them. The sequence where Leatherface makes his screen debut and offs his first two victims lasts over five minutes and is played out in real time. We are then taken on a breathless five minute chase after Leatherface lunges out of the darkness at Sally and Franklin, with no respite from that first reveal to the moment that Sally collapses in the gas station, believing herself to be safe.

Hooper's greatest achievement with The Texas Chain Saw Massacre, though, is that he manages to perfectly embody the 'less is more' maxim. Over the years many a viewer has described in great detail scenes they think they have seen in the movie, but which thanks to Hooper's masterful direction exist only in their mind. Upon my initial viewing I too was convinced that I had seen much more than I actually had, but in fact for all the gruesome goings on, we see very little explicit detail. Much is implied and left to our imagination, which is more than capable of applying the old two plus two equals five equation.

This movie, along with Carrie and The Thing, had a tremendous impact on me and remains one of the most important horror movies that I have ever seen. Definitely one that consistently makes my top ten movies list, not just within the horror genre but of all time. An essential Saturday Night Fright Flick.

**My Favourite Scene**

Hearing a generator and thinking that they may be able to score some gasoline, Kirk and Pam set off to investigate an old house they spy on the horizon. Upon reaching it Kirk annoys

Pam by giving her a tooth he finds on the stoop, and so enters the house alone after receiving no answer to his shouted greetings. Through a doorway at the end of the hall he sees numerous skulls mounted on the wall and hears what appears to be the squealing of a pig. He walks over to investigate but stumbles on a small ramp.

When Kirk looks up, Leatherface leers into view, sledgehammer raised, and smashes him on the head with a sickening thud. He drops to the floor, and we get a close up of his twitching head and kicking feet before Leatherface hits him again for good measure before dragging him through the doorway, slamming a steel shutter behind them.

Hearing the shutter slam, Pam ventures into the house looking for Kirk and stumbles into a room littered with bones. A chicken is crammed into a tiny cage, and there are pieces of furniture fashioned from actual body parts. Horrified she runs into the hallway as the steel shutter is pulled open and Leatherface runs out after her, scooping her up as she reaches the screen door and carrying her back into his workshop where he impales her on a meat hook. From here she watches as he sets to work on Kirk's body with a chainsaw.

The whole sequence lasts a little over five minutes but once seen is never forgotten. The violence, when it finally comes, happens quickly and is a massive jolt to the senses after the relative tranquillity of the movie up to this point.

For my money, this is one of the most effective and memorable entrances of a movie villain in any genre, horror or otherwise.

**Did You Know That...**

Many of the scenes in which Marilyn Burns is crying and near hysterical were genuine, as Tobe Hooper insisted on multiple takes which wore her down mentally and physically.

Early titles for the movie included 'Headcheese', 'Leatherface' and 'Stalking Leatherface'.

Tobe Hooper got the idea for the movie while standing in the hardware section in a crowded store. Thinking of a way to get out of the store quickly he spotted the chainsaw section and his imagination was fired up. Fortunately for the shoppers the chainsaw wasn't.

Gunnar Hansen only had one shirt for Leatherface's costume, and as it had been dyed it couldn't be washed. Unsurprisingly, by the end of the four-week shoot in the hot Texas summer no one wanted to eat lunch with him.

Despite the movie's title, only one person is actually killed with a chainsaw.

The movie was remade in 2003, and turned out to be one of the better remakes of the decade so far. It also spawned a prequel, Texas Chain-Saw Massacre : The Beginning in 2006 which was essentially a rerun of the remake, but still fairly entertaining.

# The Thing (1982)

Directed by:   John Carpenter
Written by:    Bill Lancaster (based on John W Campbell Jr's
                  story 'Who Goes There?')
Starring:       Kurt Russell – MacReady
                  A Wilford Brimley – Dr Blair
                  T K Carter – Nauls
                  David Clennon – Palmer
                  Keith David – Childs
                  Richard Dysart – Dr Copper
                  Charles Hallahan – Norris
                  Peter Maloney – Bennings
                  Richard Masur – Clark
                  Donald Moffat – Garry
                  Joel Polis – Fuchs
                  Thomas Waites - Windows

## Synopsis

A team of twelve men at an Antarctic research station take in a dog after the Norwegian helicopter that was pursuing and shooting at it is subsequently destroyed. After exploring the devastated Norwegian camp, however, they discover that they may have taken in something far more deadly.

Paranoia sets in as they realise that an alien that can assume the shape and appearance of any host it desires is among them. As the creature picks them off they try to discover who has been infected and who can be trusted.

## Why I Love This Movie

In 1982 John Carpenter was arguably the most famous and popular horror movie director in the world. Beginning with 1978's genre defining Halloween, Carpenter had a run of successful films including 1980's The Fog and 1981's Escape From New York that have all gone on to acquire legendary status. Though this run came to an end with The Thing, Carpenter's inspired and brilliantly executed remake of Christian Nyby's 1951 The Thing From Another World, it couldn't have ended on a higher note.

I first saw The Thing one rainy afternoon in 1983 in the British seaside town of Bexhill-on-Sea where I was on holiday with my friend Nick and his family. Thanks to the precipitous weather, Nick's dad took us to the local video rental store to get a couple of movies. Already being regular Fangoria readers at this early age, we were aware of two movies that had just been released on video and that we desperately wanted to see.

As luck would have it the video store had both of them, so after filling out a membership form, Nick's dad rented Zombie Flesh Eaters and The Thing and we hurried home, unaware that the day's viewing was about to leave a lasting impression on us. We fed the video cassette into the enormous machine, pressed play (no remote control in those days), and settled down on the sofa to watch the movie.

Back then, The Thing was completely unlike any other horror movie that I had ever seen. Until now these had usually fallen into one of two categories, either involving nubile teenagers being pursued by maniacs, masked or otherwise, or involving nubile teenagers being pursued by freakish non-human creatures, including, but not limited to, zombies, gelatinous blobs and flying piranhas.

The Thing, though, was very different. There wasn't a single nubile teenager to be seen, and in fact not a single woman. This was a tale of twelve men effectively locked up together at the bottom of the world and their relationships with each other.

Writer Bill Lancaster did a fantastic job of breathing life into the men, each of them discernably different from the other, from Nauls, the good natured roller-skating cook, to head honcho Garry who isn't up to the task of leading his men, and who garners no respect from them, to the enigmatic and reluctant helicopter pilot MacReady, who prefers his own company but when push comes to shove steps up to the plate and takes charge.

I love the way Kurt Russell brings MacReady to life – from the first time we see him losing to a game of computer chess and responding by pouring his whisky into the machines innards, to his ignorant shout of "Hey Sweden" at the Norwegian camp, which is quickly corrected by Doc Copper, who gives him a patient, almost fatherly look and tells him "They're not Swedish, Mac, they're Norwegian".

Akin to an alternate reality version of Snake Plisskin, MacReady is a reluctant hero, thrust into the role of leader almost by default. From the first alien transformation in the dog pen when he sends for the flamethrower, Mac is the real head honcho. Though Garry might walk around with his revolver slung at his hip like some modern day cowboy, it is Mac in his battered Stetson who exudes that leadership quality and who commands the respect of the men.

In my opinion, MacReady is one of Kurt Russell's finest turns. Not as cool as Snake, and not as entertaining as Jack Burton, Big Trouble In Little China's reluctant hero (hmmm, spotting a pattern here), MacReady is nevertheless utterly believable. His mannerisms and interactions with the other eleven men are completely credible, helped largely by the fact that each of them are well drawn characters you can imagine as real people as opposed to the movie stereotypes that many horror movies defer to – the jock, the pothead, the smart one, yadda yadda yadda.

It is this sense of the ordinary and the realistic interaction between the men that is at the heart of The Thing's real horror. Though the first thing that comes to mind whenever this movie is mentioned are the special effects, and they are stunning, more of which in a moment, this is not so much a movie about a bloody, murderous alien creature as it is about the way human beings are quick to resort to paranoia and turn on one another when threatened with the unknown.

The moment that the truth about the alien organism is revealed, that it can imitate any one of them, any trust they may have had in each other quickly evaporates. Carpenter cleverly draws us, the viewer, into this as well, by never showing us who is next up to be assimilated. There is no nod to the audience or aside to let us in on the secret here. Instead we only find out who is not quite themselves anymore at the same time as the rest of the men do, and this makes for a very tense and ultimately very satisfying ride.

The Thing's crowning achievement for me, though, and the reason it has been one of my all time favourite movies for so many years is that in the annals of celluloid history it will forever be revered as the movie that completely smashed the mould as to what could be achieved with puppets, gelatin and kayro syrup It stands now in this modern age of CGI effects as a testament to what was achievable in the 'good old days' of doing everything 'for real', a reminder that however good your CGI is, there will never be a better substitute for 'real' creature effects.

Take spiders, for example. Shelob scared the pants off me in Peter Jackson's Lord of the Rings : The Return of the King, but she came nowhere near evoking the sense of disgust and unease that I felt at watching the Norris spider-head sprout legs and scuttle off down the corridor, accompanied by the immortal line "You've got to be fucking kidding!"

It's incredible to think that Rob Bottin, the genius behind the groundbreaking effects, was only 22 years old at the time, and virtually lived at the studio, such was the intense pressure to come up with the design and execution of the effects that have since gone down in movie history. Nothing I had seen before and very little I have seen since comes even close to the awe that the first viewing of The Thing instilled in me. Once the film was over I remember rewinding it to the scene with Norris and replaying it over and over while trying to figure out just how the hell they did it. Thanks to the wonders of DVD extras and commentary tracks I now know exactly how Rob Bottin pulled it off, but back then it was quite literally movie magic.

Even so, when watching it again for this book I found I was still sitting there open-mouthed at the set pieces. The first transformation, which was actually pulled off by effects grandmaster Stan Winston, brought in as a favour for the exhausted Bottin, still completely amazes me. There is more imagination in that single scene than in the whole running time of many other movies, and this is just the start of The Thing's rampage. From the splitting open of the dog's head to the huge grotesque claws that push their way out through the roof, it's hard to lift your jaw from the ground for a single second between those two visuals.

A truly great ensemble piece and perhaps the last great non-CGI horror movie, The Thing feels fresh even after numerous viewings, and thanks to its remote setting and totally believable cast will never truly age, apart from perhaps the now primitive chess computer that MacReady plays with at the start of the film. The game is symbolically reprised in the final shots of the movie as the two surviving men size each other up and try and decide whether either, or neither, of them has been assimilated by The Thing. A classic bleak ending that works perfectly.

The last word must go to Jed, the half wolf / half husky who plays the original incarnation of The Thing. I've seen many animals in movies over the years, but this dog truly seems to be acting. His every look and nuance is almost as if he himself is a CGI character, and he manages to portray the brooding, patient intelligence of the creature perfectly. Just one more immaculate detail in what I consider to be a near perfect movie. If you haven't seen this classic, then make it your next DVD purchase because they really don't make them like this anymore.

## My Favourite Scene

It's a close call between the dog pen transformation and the Norris sequence, but for the sheer jaw dropping factor the latter wins hands down. It would have been more than enough to have ended the scene after the Norris thing had bitten the Doc's arms off and then erupted into the twisted flesh and bone creation that forced its way out of its chest, but no. On top of that we got the stunning sight of his head stretching its way off his body and onto the floor, and then sprouting eight legs and two eyestalks before scuttling away down the corridor.

I can honestly say that I have seen nothing since that has made my jaw drop like this whole sequence did.

## Did You Know That...

Donald Pleasance was Carpernter's first choice for the character of Blair, but had to decline due to scheduling conflicts.

The main titles were shot using a fish tank with smoke in it, with the letters drawn on an animation cell, behind which was a sheet of garbage bag plastic stretched across a frame. When flames heated the plastic, it melted away and allowed the light to shine through the letters.

The female voice of MacReady's chess computer is that of Adrienne Barbeau, Carpenter's then wife, and most famous for her turn as DJ Stevie Wayne in his 1980 movie The Fog.

The video that the men watch of the Norwegian crew finding the spacecraft beneath the ice is actually footage from Christian Nyby's The Thing From Another World.

The original 1951 movie took place at the North Pole, whereas Carpenter's remake takes place at the South Pole.

An alternative ending was shot showing MacReady having a blood test that confirms that he is not affected, but this was only ever done as a safety net in case the studio didn't like the original ending, and to this day both Carpenter and Russell confirm that even they don't know which, if either, of the two men has been replaced by The Thing and when.

# Wolf Creek (2005)

Directed by:   Greg McLean
Written by:   Greg McLean
Starring:     John Jarrat – Mick Taylor
              Cassandra Magrath – Liz Hunter
              Kestie Morassi – Kristy Earl
              Nathan Phillips – Ben Mitchell

**Synopsis**

Two English girls and an Australian boy set off on a cross-country journey across Australia, stopping off at the Wolf Creek meteor crater along the way. Returning to their car they find that it won't start, but luckily a friendly man turns up with a truck and offers to help them fix it back at his home.

Once at his compound, however, it becomes apparent that he may not be the Samaritan he initially seemed to be.

**Why I Love This Movie**

Early in 2005 I became aware through stirrings on the Arrow In The Head site and in Fangoria that a little low budget movie lensed in Australia was all set to make some significant waves in the horror community. The intriguingly titled Wolf Creek was apparently going to knock our socks off in terms of terror and so, being the genre fan that I am, this news grabbed my attention.

Fangoria subsequently ran an article on it that gave little away in terms of the plot, but even so there was a groundswell of expectation building up that I hadn't experienced since the days of the Blair Witch hype a decade earlier. Finally Wolf Creek was given a release date here in the UK and I got my chance to judge it for myself. I wasn't disappointed.

Writer and director Greg McLean delivered a movie that hit all of my favourite buttons – a remote location, a chilling villain, and that rarest of commodities in the current climate of rent-a-teen horror movies, characters that actually felt like real people and that I could invest some emotional currency in.

Casandra Magrath, Kestie Morassi and Nathan Phillips infused their characters with a realism that I hadn't seen on screen for a long time. The chemistry between them, given ample time to breathe in the slow burning first half of the movie, is impeccable, and I found myself completely believing in them, and their relationships with one another.

Magrath and Morassi, as Liz and Kristy, particularly impressed me with their impressive command of the English accent. Being a Brit myself it takes a lot to impress me when a foreign tongue tackles it, but they actually had me convinced that they *were* English actresses until I saw the DVD extras and discovered that they were actually both Australian born and bred.

Phillips, too, was a revelation, breathing life into his Australian character by deftly avoiding all of the clichés and stereotypes that three decades of Aussie soaps have foisted on the world, and instead giving us a boy who is by turns confident and bashful. He also delivers a solitary moment of comic genius in the movie when harassed by a group of tattooed, burly men in a rest stop.

One of the men asks him whether he minds if they have a gang bang with his two girls, at which point he turns away and mutters "dickhead". The man stands up, a good foot and a half taller than Ben and asks him what he just said. Full of piss and vinegar Ben turns around to defend his comment but seeing the magnitude of his potential problem quickly changes his tune and instead meekly replies, "That's a nice smile you've got there".

Though very much a slow burner, the fact that McLean invests so much time in letting us get to know the three leads, and as a result growing to care about what is in store for them, means that the movie pays off magnificently in the second half when everything goes to hell. When bad things begin to happen to these three kids I was very much bothered about their well-being.

As likable and believable as the main characters are, though, a successful horror movie is nothing without a genuinely chilling villain, and Wolf Creek delivers in spades. Being set firmly in reality, no Freddys, Jasons or Pinheads here, the maniac of Wolf Creek is a regular flesh and blood man, much like The Stepfather's Jerry Blake, which is, for me, an absolutely frightening and disturbing proposition.

Mick Taylor, played with extreme relish by veteran actor John Jarrat, is a charming, likeable, easy going and funny man who on the surface comes across as the more roguish, gone-to-seed older brother of Mick 'Crocodile' Dundee. Director McLean even goes so far as to include some seemingly throwaway dialogue referencing the "that's not a knife, *this* is a knife" catchphrase of Paul Hogan's popular 1980s movies.

Unfortunately for our travellers he is also a sadistic, nasty, utterly remorseless man who delights in the torture and torment of whoever is unlucky enough to stray into his orbit. Mick Taylor is undoubtedly one of the most unsettling movie villains that I've ever come across because of the sheer pleasure that he derives from his actions. Every moment of his twisted existence is a blast for Taylor as he plays with his victims.

After drugging our three travellers, he ties one of them to a pole in his 'torture room' and to the soundtrack of her cries and pleadings loads a high-powered rifle before aiming it at her. As she pleads with him he suddenly yells "bang!" and collapses in hysterical laughter, a two note low guttural laugh that brings to mind John Williams's extremely effective theme from Jaws, highly amused at his little joke.

It is this sheer single mindedness that I love about Mick Taylor, and which has swiftly catapulted him into my personal top ten of movie villains. Jarret himself considers Taylor his most accomplished role in a long and distinguished career, and I have to agree with him. There is something about villains who could literally live next door to you, and who seem to be, on the surface anyway, likeable and friendly. These are the worst kind to come across in real life, just ask the neighbours of John Wayne Gacy who regularly dressed as a clown to raise money for children's charities and who was photographed shaking hands with not one but two American Presidents as a result of his fundraising efforts, but in the movies they ring my bell every time.

The real star of the movie, though, doesn't even appear in the credits despite being on screen for much of the running time. As eminently watchable as the four leads are, they pale into insignificance next to the absolutely stunning panoramas and landscapes of the Australian outback that McLean shares with us.

Bringing to mind the beautiful imagery of Richard Stanley's much underrated 1992 movie Dust Devil, and also Peter Weir's classic 1975 flick Picnic At Hanging Rock, Wolf Creek is stuffed to the gills with jaw dropping visuals. From shots of the sun sinking slowly below the desert horizon, to a flock of white birds taking flight from a group of trees, to a simply breathtaking lunar eclipse, McLean confidently and effectively conveys the scale of the emptiness that the three leads find themselves in the middle of.

It is precisely this sense of isolation that successfully underpins the seriousness of the situation that Kris, Liz and Ben find themselves in. It subconsciously places the realisation at the back of our minds that even if they do get away from Mick Taylor, there is literally no help around for tens if not hundreds of miles.

By doing this, McLean conveys to people in countries like my own, England, where no matter how far into the so called wilderness you go you are never more than a couple of hours

162

drive away from so called civilisation, that these kids are literally stranded in the middle of nowhere.

Though the visuals might seem perfectly at home in a National Geographical documentary, once the movie reaches the halfway mark and takes a sharp left into dark territory, a roadmap it shares with Eli Roth's 2006 flick Hostel, Wolf Creek really earns its reputation as an uncompromising genre movie.

As the second half unfolds, the extent of Mick Taylor's madness and sadism becomes more and more apparent, as each of the three travellers are put through ordeals that are both brutal and unsettling.

Not to give too much away (and avoid this paragraph and also my favourite scene if you haven't yet seen this movie and intend to), Taylor elevates himself into the annals of the most twisted and sadistic killers as he deals with each of the three leads. This movie is definitely not from the 'less is more' school and earns its bloody stripes with honours in one particular scene (described in detail in my favourite scene) that ranks as one of the most original and brutal scenes that I've seen in a long time.

For me, though, the power of this movie isn't derived from the visceral scenes alone. Much of the impact, and what makes Wolf Creek such a watchable flick, is that McLean shoots a lot of the movie in extreme close up, putting us, the viewer, in an uncomfortably voyeuristic position as we are privy to the conversations and experiences of the three travellers.

In one extended scene we ride in their car with them as Taylor tows them back to his compound, experiencing their reservations and fears about their situation. In another we explore his storeroom, full of artefacts that he has collected from previous victims, which reminded me of similar scenes in Alexandre Aja's 2006 remake of The Hills have Eyes and the much underrated Kurt Russell thriller Breakdown.

We watch as the character involved finds numerous photographs and driving licences pinned to Taylor's wall. We are then privy to recordings on two video cameras, the first of which shows Taylor pulling the exact same rescue trick on a young family that he has just used on our three friends, and the second being Ben's footage which reveals that their meeting with Taylor wasn't as random as we, or they, first believed.

Wolf Creek is a breath of fresh air in the PG13 world of horror, a movie that isn't afraid to be an uncompromising horror flick, and one that delivers genuine feelings of unease, tension and repulsion. The most disturbing aspect of the movie, however, is that it is based on an amalgamation of several real life cases, some of which, as director McLean reveals in the making of feature on the DVD, are are even more horrific than the events portrayed in the movie.

Unlike the tenuous 'based on a true story' claims of Tobe Hooper's 1974 Texas Chain Saw Massacre (which was actually very loosely based on the crimes of Plainfield resident Ed Gein, as was Robert Bloch's Psycho novel, filmed of course by Alfred Hitchcock), the events of McLean's movie are very much rooted in reality. Drawing heavily on the notorious Backpacker Murders case in which Ivan Milat was convicted of murdering eight tourists in New South Wales in the 1990s, McLean's movie acts as a very effective cautionary tale for prospective backpackers. As a consequence, I currently have no plans to discover the wonders of Australia's outback.

**My Favourite Scene**

Having seen many, many killings on screen over the years I thought I'd seen pretty much seen every possible permutation of murder. However, McLean hit a home run by including a highly original and visceral scene in Wolf Creek that I had never come across before. This isn't the only reason it's my favourite scene in the movie, though. That honour is bestowed because it is a fantastically nasty and effective scene in its own right. (Skip this section now if you haven't seen the movie!)

Thinking she's home free having located some car keys, Liz slides behind the wheel of one of Taylor's many cars. However, he is waiting for her in the back and plunges a knife through the seat and her.

Crawling out of the car and cowering on the floor, Taylor follows and stands above her as she brandishes a Swiss Army knife at him. He responds with Crocodile Dundee's quote that *"this is a knife"* and swings his huge blade at her, severing three of her fingers.

He then tells her of a procedure used in the Vietnamese war to prevent prisoners escaping and after administering a vicious headbutt ("that's for wreckin' me truck") plunges his knife, accompanied by some deliciously visceral sounds, into her back, severing her spinal column and creating a 'head on a stick'.

Though a brief scene, it turns everything we thought we knew on its head. Up to this point Liz had seemed to be the obvious Final Girl, but with this act of brutal violence all bets were off.

**Did You Know That**

The name of the abandoned mining company that is home to Mick Taylor's compound, the Navithalim Mining Co, is actually the name of notorious Australian backpacker murderer Ivan Milat spelt backwards (well, almost!)

The abandoned mine where the movie was shot was, unbeknownst to the crew, the site of a real life murder.

The crater at Wolf Creek in the movie is a real crater, but spelt slightly differently – "Wolfe Creek".

Both Nathan Phillips and Kestie Morassi had previously appeared in Australian soap opera Neighbours in the 1990s.

# Wrong Turn (2003)

Directed by:   Rob Schmidt
Written by:    Alan B McElroy
Starring:      Desmond Harrington – Chris Flynn
              Eliza Dushku – Jessie Burlingame
              Emmanuelle Chriqui – Carly
              Jeremy Sisto – Scott
              Kevin Zegers – Evan
              Lindy Booth – Francine

## Synopsis

Late for an interview and held up by an accident on the freeway, Chris Flynn decides to take a short cut down an old dirt road. After taking his eyes off the road for a moment, he rounds a bend and crashes into a truck whose tyres have been blown out by a booby trap.

Hooking up with the five other stranded teens from the truck, they try to find help but soon discover that the backwoods of North Virginia are not the friendliest of places.

## Why I Love This Movie

When Wrong Turn first started getting coverage in the likes of Fangoria I was more than a little excited. Director Rob Schmidt was promising a return to the gut-wrenching no holds barred horror movies of the 1970s as an antidote to the teen-friendly fare that had been clogging up the genre since the advent of the Scream movies in 1986. Now don't get me wrong, I love a lot of the movies that came out of this whole 'ironic' sub-genre, but being a child of the 1980s horror scene I'd been hankering for a return to good old fashioned visceral movies for a while by this point. On top of this, special effects legend Stan Winston was on board and enthusing like mad about the project, even going so far as to promise to show us things we'd never seen before, which to give him his due he managed with at least one scene, more of which later.

While the story is nothing new, teenagers get stranded in the backwoods and are stalked by a bunch of inbred, deformed good ol' boys with a taste for human casseroles, Schmidt delivers a film that gives several nods to its forerunners, and yet still manages to keep us fully entertained for the movie's lean eighty minute running time.

The film starts as it means to go on, with a couple of climbers falling foul of some unseen, but obviously violent and disturbed assailant who clubs and throws one of them off a cliff, and drags the other off to a fate likely to be worse than death. Cutting to Desmond Harrington's character, Chris, who initially comes across as your common or garden teen slasher movie victim, we watch as he sets off into the backwoods to find a way around the chemical spill that's going to make him late for an interview, stopping at a run down gas station for directions.

For those of us above a certain age the old déjà vu bells begin ringing at this point as we survey the scene. Run down gas station? Check. Ugly attendant with dirty overalls and bad teeth? Check. Greasy barbeque rotisserie with odd shaped pieces of meat? Well, not in this case, but we do get a nice bubbling stew pot later on in the movie containing pieces of meat of undeterminable origin, but for now two out of three clichés ain't bad.

It does make you wonder whether it's an unwritten law, mainly because writing never seems high on the agenda with these, ahem, special communities, that the least deformed or insane member of the clan has to own a gas station and direct the unsuspecting general public into their misshapen clutches. It must work, though, as there always seems to be a decent sized example of another of the genre's clichés, the vehicle graveyard, which suggests that business is reasonably good.

Funnily enough, though, rather than take anything away from the movie, it is the embracing of these clichés, particularly in the first half, that endears it to me. Though it wears its obvious influences on its sleeve, namely the original Texas Chain Saw Massacre and John Boorman's 1972 classic Deliverance, which is actually name checked as Desmond Harrington's character is about to let himself into an old run down cabin and is told by Jeremy Sisto "I need to remind you of a little movie called Deliverance", Wrong Turn does it with such reverence and style that it's easy to forgive the fact that you've seen this all before.

Or at least you think you have. Rather than serve up the old tired clichéd characters, Schmidt actually gives us four people that we can care about. Granted there are six teens initially, but the two stoner characters are quickly offed before they can become too annoying, one of them in a very brutal fashion, leaving us with a recently engaged couple, and two singletons who you'd have to be blind not to see the potential bonding being telegraphed even at this early stage of the movie.

I've often wondered if there's some sort of IKEA for backwoods folk that ensures that every run down cabin or derelict house you visit looks exactly the same. When our teens find the inevitable run down cabin in this movie, rather than groaning, I personally got a kick out of mentally ticking off the essential furnishings as they explored it. In no particular order we get several plates of spoiled food, a smorgasbord of sharp, rusty implements, the obligatory heart-wrenching music box that plays a twee tune, a small tiara, the inevitable cooking pot full of who knows what (or who), a bathtub full of dirty water with a hand sticking out of it, a pile of cheap sunglasses and my favourite, a jar full of false teeth. And that's before we get to the fridge.

As Chris opens said appliance we discover shelf upon shelf of transparent Tupperware containers full of delicacies not on sale at your local delicatessen and one very conspicuous tub made from opaque plastic. Apparently having not seen enough, Mr Curious just has to open this one and we're treated to the sight of a joint of meat that will in all probability taste a little like chicken if popular wisdom is to be believed.

The interior decorating wasn't the only homage to the old days, though. True to their word, Messrs Schmidt and Winston delivered plenty of the red stuff including a nasty barbed chain/mouth interface, a couple of nice arrow impacts, including one that'll make you jump coming out of the blue but shown in all its glory, not one but two slow panning shots of a hacked up body on a table and a very inventive and original kill that I'll get to in a minute.

There's also a couple of off-screen actions that just like the original Texas Chain-Saw Massacre make you think you've seen more than you really have, including a sequence with a leg, a saw and some very squishy sound effects, and another Argento-esque shot that tracks into a keyhole where we see a close up of an eyeball in which the reflection of one of our mountain men hacking up a victim can be seen. Very stylish and extremely effective.

What sets this movie aside from being just a rehash of the old 1970s clichés is that fact that in the second half it pulls a couple of very original ideas out of the bag. After being almost caught in the cabin by the three mountain men, and being forced to witness their unique cooking preparations, the four survivors head off into the deep woods. So far, so clichéd. However after being pared down to a trio, the three teens take the movie quite literally to a higher level. Discovering a watchtower, the movie suddenly veers into original territory as they climb high above the tree line in search of a radio and a safe haven.

After showing such intellectual promise, they then do something really dumb considering they're trying to hide (I never said the movie was perfect, just entertaining) and it's the mountain men's turn to show a spark of initiative. This results in our kids finding themselves performing a hire wire act in the tree tops along with one of the freaks, and setting up the best scene in the movie which also happens to be one of the best kills I'd seen for a long time.

Another reason this movie works so well for me, and is one I can watch repeatedly, is the characters themselves. Yes, they're teens and this is for all intents and purposes a teen stalk and slash movie, but thanks to a likeable cast, including Desmond Harrington who I first came across in 2001's superb psychological thriller The Hole (and who excelled in 2003's little seen Love Object), Eliza Dushku, better known as Buffy The Vampire Slayer's nemesis Faith, and Jeremy Sisto who was superb in HBO's Six Feet Under, I found myself actually giving a damn about these people.

Also worth mentioning is the title sequence, which is a perfect example in how to effectively and quickly set up a background story using visuals alone. Over the space of a couple of minutes, we are shown a montage of yellowing pictures of deformed people interspersed with newspaper articles on inbreeding and mountain men, and shots of missing posters and reports, all of which tell us everything we need to know for the following hour or so. I personally think it's up there with the best opening titles of the last couple of decades, sharing the accolade with David Fincher's titles for 1995's Se7en and Wes Craven's montage of Freddy Krueger constructing his trademark glove from 1984's A Nightmare On Elm Street. Director Alexandre Aja obviously agreed as well, as he borrowed heavily from the idea for the titles for his 2006 remake of The Hills Have Eyes.

To conclude, Wrong Turn may not be the most original or perfect horror movie ever made, but it is undeniably good fun, and no matter how many times I see it always entertains me. It also quietly began to pave the way for the mid-naughties renaissance of dark, bloody and violent horror movies that have included the likes of Eli Roth's Hostel, Alexandre Aja's aforementioned remake of Wes Craven's The Hills Have Eyes and Rob Zombie's underrated The Devil's Rejects.

## My Favourite Scene

After narrowly escaping being barbecued in the watchtower, our survivors find themselves high in the trees, balancing on thin boughs as the torch wielding mountain men fire arrows up at them from the ground. One of our surviving teens finds herself faltering at the prospect of walking along a narrow branch and backs against the tree trunk as one of the mountain men rises into frame behind her, axe in hand.

As the other two watch from the other end of the bough, he slams the axe into her face, pinning her to the tree through the mouth. A close up on her eyeball follows, the pupil growing larger as the camera pulls back and up to watch her body tumble down through the trees, leaving the upper half of her head balancing on the axe embedded in the tree trunk.

Though the body falling away from us is an obvious CGI shot, the top of the head is real (and still very much attached to the actress) giving the sequence a convincing look and the execution, pun fully intended, is superb, making good on Stan Winston's promise of showing us something we hadn't seen before. Definitely one of the most inventive kills I've seen over the years.

## Did You Know That...

Eliza Dushku's character Jessie Burlingame is named after the lead character in Stephen King's novel Gerald's Game.

Desmond Harrington broke his right ankle during filming, which made shooting some of his scenes somewhat difficult as his character had been shot in the left leg and had to limp on his right foot.

At the time of release the MPAA (Motion Picture Association of America) deemed the majority of the TV spots and trailers to be 'too intense' for viewers, requiring the commercials to be heavily trimmed.

Garry Robbins, who played 'Saw-Tooth', is 7'1" and was at one time a Canadian professional wrestler known as the 'Paul Bunyan of the North'.

Lindy Booth appeared in Zack Snyder's 2004 remake of Dawn of the Dead.

# Zombie Flesh Eaters (1979)

Directed by:   Lucio Fulci
Written by:    Elisa Briganti
Starring:       Tisa Farrow – Anne Bowles
                Ian McCulloch – Peter West
                Richard Johnson – Dr David Menard
                Al Cliver – Brian Hull
                Auretta Gay – Susan Barrett
                Stefania D'Amario – Missey
                Olga Karlatos – Paola Menard

## Synopsis

After a zombie is found in New York harbour on a boat belonging to a respected doctor, a reporter teams up with the missing man's daughter to find him.

They travel with another couple on their boat to Matul Island where they manage to locate a friend and colleague of her father, but find him fighting a losing battle with a virus that is bringing the dead back to life.

As the island becomes overrun with zombies, they desperately try to find a way off it before they become lunch.

## Why I Love This Movie

Zombie Flesh Eaters will always have a very special place in my heart as part of the double bill, along with John Carpenter's

The Thing, that my friend Nick and I watched on that fateful rainy afternoon in Bexhill-on-Sea in 1983.

As I have already mentioned in the review of The Thing, that afternoon was to blow our minds in the form of a double whammy of movies that to this day both conjure up visions of the first time I saw them.

Whereas I knew something of The Thing's plot thanks to having read the novelization by Allen Dean Foster (who also did the honours on Alien and Disney's The Black Hole), Zombie Flesh Eaters was completely virgin territory.

It seems incredible in today's age of the internet, particularly sites like Ain't It Cool News and John Fallon's superb Arrow in the Head, that a horror movie fan could be unaware of anything coming down the pipe, but back then unless you could get your hands on a copy of Fangoria, which was no mean feat in England, then you had to rely on good old word of mouth, or your friend's Dad who loved seeing these 'X' rated flicks at the cinema.

The thing I truly love about Fulci's best-known movie is that right from the start it grabs you by the throat and then doesn't let go until the end credits roll. Within the first fifteen seconds of the movie, we have had a gun pointed out of the screen at us, and seen an unidentified man shoot a body that is rising from a bed, wrapped in a white sheet and tied securely with rope, in the head. Fulci then zooms in to show us the ruined brain matter protruding through the bullet hole.

As far as getting things off to a literal bang this is one of the most effective openings I have ever seen, and even now having just watched the movie for the umpteenth time for this book, it still brings a twisted smile to my face.

Unlike many of the numerous zombie movies that littered the video stores in the 80s, Zombie Flesh Eaters somehow managed to get everything right, and proves that like his fellow Italian Dario Argento, Fulci could bring a distinctive and very effective style to the screen.

The opening shots of the boat floating adrift just off New York's Staten Island are both panoramic when Fulci uses wide angles to frame the boat against the distinctive backdrops of the World Trade Centre and the Statue of Liberty, and unsettling when he moves in tight on the boat, shooting from unusual angles to throw us off balance.

Later in the movie his shots of the village on Matul Island send shivers up the spine as he again uses wide angles to show dusty, deserted streets, save for the occasional wild dog or scuttling crab, accompanied by the low moaning of the wind. A variation on this appears towards the end of the movie as Fulci gives us a lovely long and wide shot of a road full of zombies, slowly shuffling towards camera.

His crowning glory, though, is a stunningly beautiful underwater sequence involving a topless diver (naturally, this was the exploitative 80s after all), a large shark and a zombie. For a low budget, supposedly 'spaghetti horror' movie, this sequence alone deserves much more praise than it has garnered over the years, and is in fact my favourite scene in the movie, more of which later.

Sadly Fulci's wonderful cinematography and the fact that Zombie Flesh Eaters actually had a surprisingly intelligent script were completely overlooked in the furore over the so-called 'Video Nasties' witch hunt that was led by the Daily Mail newspaper, outraged that children (like Nick and I) might be seeing this 'evil' movie.

While many of the zombie movies, and even George A Romero's trilogy, offered no explanation as to why the dead were rising and feeling peckish, writer Elisa Briganti set up a convincing dilemma for the character of Doctor Menard. As a man of science, he desperately searches for a rational, scientific explanation for the walking dead, refusing to believe the rumours that voodoo is at the heart of the outbreak.

The movie also delivers a bleak look at the little seen gestation period between infection and death, taking us inside Menard's makeshift hospital among the dirty, bloodied sheets on which his patients are securely tied to their beds as he tries in vain to help them.

This brief and rare glimpse of the suffering and terror that the victims go through before they become zombies is crowned by a scene in which Menard's friend, Anne's father, begs him to ensure that his soul rests in peace, and the subsequent struggle that Menard has with himself before shooting him in the head as his corpse reanimates. Pathos for the undead. Who'd have thought in a 'spaghetti horror'?

A zombie movie wouldn't be complete without a decent amount of gore, and again Fulci delivers here, in spades. One of my favourite scenes in any zombie movie, and incidentally one of the most infamous scenes in just about any horror movie of the last three decades, find's Menard's wife's eyeball on the receiving end of a sharp splinter.

To this day the uncut version of this scene is unavailable in my home country of England (though I do, of course, have an imported complete print of the movie), but I have a distinct memory of my friend Bridget actually running from the room when she first saw it and throwing her dinner up into the toilet. Fulci would have been proud.

The first time I saw this scene I remember sitting with my mouth open as Fulci employed his favourite trick of utilising point of view shots to put you in the shoes of the victim. He cut between close-ups of Mrs Menard's eye and the sharp splinter slowly approaching our eyes until the two met and to my surprise at the time, he actually showed it being driven deep into her eye! On screen!

While this has become the most talked about scene in the movie over the years, the rest of the running time is filled with a decent number of exploding heads (literally in one instance), torn out throats, severed fingers, geysers of blood from various wounds, and the titular flesh eating as a group of zombies chow down on what is left of Mrs Menard's body in a scene that also, sadly, remains off the menu in the UK version.

However, while the gore is a plus point to those of us who like the red stuff, the movie works superbly on the suspense level as well, much of which is attributable to Giorgio Cascio and Fabio Frizzi's distinctive and memorable score. The main Zombie Flesh Eaters theme is a hypnotic drum and synthesiser piece that I absolutely love to this day, and is perhaps the most recognisable piece of horror movie music ever produced.

It perfectly creates an atmosphere of tension and unease, and Fulci is clever in using it sparingly to maximise its effect, filling much of the rest of the soundtrack with the rhythmic and relentlessly oppressive sound of jungle drums. By doing so he raises the bar as far as keeping the audience on edge and feeling slightly uneasy.

Watching the movie again for the purposes of researching this book, I was pleasantly surprised at just how terrifying the zombies of old were. Though they moved so sluggishly that you could literally outcrawl them, their singular purpose, excruciatingly slow shuffling gait and lack of expression makes them so much more frightening than the current crop of Zack Snyder and Danny Boyle's undead sprinters.

Don't get me wrong, I think the new breed of zombies are interesting and do add something to the whole mythology, but in my eyes you can't beat the undead from back in the day. Romero's Hare Krishna zombie from Dawn of the Dead wouldn't have been half as menacing if he'd legged it down the corridor instead of jerkily turning like a toy with dying batteries, and Day of the Dead's Bub would've looked just plain wrong speed saluting Captain Rhodes after shooting him.

My favourite thing about Fulci's movie, though, is how he unashamedly rips off, or homages depending on your point of view, Romero's Dawn of the Dead from the previous year. Paraphrasing Ken Foree's famous "When there is no more room in hell, the dead will walk the Earth" line, Menard's assistant Lucas tells him that "When the Earth spits out the dead, they will come back to suck the blood from the living".

The final shot, too, leads nicely into the beginning of Dawn, as Fulci shows us a shot of the Brooklyn Bridge overrun with zombies while a radio announcer tells us first that New York is under siege from zombies, and then that he has just received a report that they have entered the building, followed by his scream. (I like to think that this might be the same studio that Dawn of the Dead's Fran and Stephen have just left.)

Zombie Flesh Eaters is, in my humble opinion, a great Saturday Night Fright Flick thanks to its intelligent script, competent acting (particularly from Ian McCulloch, better known to us Brits as the Greg Preston from the superb 1970's survival horror series Survivors), and lashings of the red stuff, even in the not quite uncut UK release. Not quite as nasty as the Daily Mail would have you believe, but still great fun.

**My Favourite Scene**

The underwater zombie versus shark scene.

Susan has gone diving to take photographs and comes across a shark. As she hides from it, a zombie attacks her. She manages to fend him off with a piece of coral and swims off, at which point he decides to take on the shark.

Zombie and shark wrestle as Fulci's camera reels around them, until the zombie tears a chunk of flesh away and stuffs it into his mouth. The shark comes back after him and they go head to head, grappling with the grace of an underwater ballet until the shark chomps down on his arm and rips it off.

The whole sequence is beautifully shot by Fulci, from the establishing shots of deep blue water and schools of fish, to the way the camera dances around the combatants. Very stylish.

**Did You Know That...**

Captain Haggerty, who played the large bald zombie on the boat at the beginning of the movie, walked into legendary punk venue CBGB's in his full zombie makeup during filming but was allegedly barely noticed.

Tisa Farrow, who plays Anne Bowles is the sister of Woody Allen's ex-wife Mia Farrow.

The movie was actually written before George A Romero's Dawn of the Dead was released in Italy, but the opening and closing scenes, which take place in New York, were added later to cash in on Dawn's success.

One of the tag lines used for the movie was the very matter of fact "We are going to eat you!"

# In Memorium

No book is written without influences, encouragement and belief, and this one is no exception. Therefore I'd like to shout out a few thank yous to some of the people who have unwittingly inspired me to put fingers to keyboard and produce the one you've just read.

First and foremost my parents, **Barbara and Tony**, who never once shied away from the fact that their first-born developed an unhealthy obsession with all things macabre and dark from a very early age, and have continued to support this bloody addiction ever since. If only they knew what they were unleashing that fateful night back in 1978.

Next up is my friend **Nick Webber**, and his dad **Michael**, with whom we shared many a Saturday afternoon watching good, bad and downright atrocious horror movies. If not for Mr Webber then I wouldn't have seen nearly as many of the old-school flicks on good old VHS as I did.

An honourable mention goes to my partner in crime **Gary Walters**, with whom I shared my obsession during the 80s and 90s. Between us we managed to obtain just about every movie on the United Kingdom's 1984 Video Recordings Act's banned list (of which quite a few we mourn the lost hours watching such complete and utter garbage), and a good many that should have been on there but weren't by virtue of the fact that they were never actually granted a UK release.

Eternal gratitude to the anonymous trader at Nottingham's Comic Fairs who always had a good supply of dodgy VHS movies that he somehow sourced from various laserdiscs throughout the world. Were it not for him then we wouldn't have been able to experience the uncut delights of the likes of Argento and Fulci so early on in our obsession.

Thank you (thank you, thank you, thank you) to **Fangoria** magazine, and to all who have written for her over the years, for being a rock solid island in the sea of gore that defines our beloved genre. Ever since discovering issue 49 in a dark and dingy newsagent in Nottingham all those years ago it has provided an insightful, in-depth and above all entertaining view of horror movies, and is essential reading to this day. (And a tearful remembrance of her short lived sister mag **Gorezone**, which was equally bold and daring, particularly with a memorable cover image of a certain head injury from **Intruder**!)

A special mention to **JoBlo**, otherwise known as **Berge Garabedian,** whose excellent book 'The 50 Coolest Movies Of All Time' inspired me to attempt this one. Check out his very cool, critically acclaimed (by Spielberg among others, no less) website at www.joblo.com

And finally, a big shout out to Berge's best friend and partner in crime **John Fallon**, aka **Arrow,** who as well as being a writer, producer and actor also runs the horror movie arm of JoBlo's site, the highly acclaimed Arrow In The Head (www.joblo.com/arrowinthehead). I became a moderator on one of the AITH forums nearly half a decade ago, and have since had the pleasure of scoring some of the music for John's movie **Deaden**. As Berge notes in his own book, John is one of the hardest working, most determined people that I know, and I am proud to be able to call him a friend. Here's to you, bud.

Cheers.

# About The Author

Ever since that fateful night in 1978 when he first saw Carrie, Richard Cosgrove has been a disciple of the horror movie, and has seen literally hundreds and hundreds of them. The Good, The Bad, and the downright atrocious (aka The Mangler).

Richard has also been a moderator on the world famous Arrow In The Head site (www.joblo.com/arrow) for nigh on half a decade, has had his short fiction included in horror anthologies, has composed music for a movie (written by and starring Arrow himself, no less), and has published a book of his black and photography, which while not horrific in itself did include a few nice shots of Parisian cemeteries.

author photograph by Deborah Gibbs

cover photograph by Richard Cosgrove

a

**production**

www.houseofdarcy.co.uk

www.houseofdarcy.co.uk/todiefor